D0995934

GREENWOOD
GUIDES

The Team

Fiona Greenwood

Simon Greenwood

Adam Barnes

Antonia Bolingbroke-Kent

Tory Gordon-Harris

First published in 2003 by Greenwood Guides,
10 Oliphant St, London W10 4EG, UK.

First edition

Copyright © May 2003 Greenwood Guides

ISBN 0-9537980-3-8 printed in China.

THE GREENWOOD GUIDE TO

CANADA

special hand-picked accommodation

www.greenwoodguides.com

Acknowledgements

Adam, Antonia and Tory were fun to live with, well organised, they wrote with great panache… and everybody seemed to like them enormously. Otherwise they were all pretty useless.

Many thanks also to Rodney Donald for his great magnanimity in allowing his house to be overrun by the Greenwood Guides and for his continued support throughout the project.

Series Editors Simon and Fiona Greenwood

Canada Editor Adam Barnes

Writing collaboration and inspections Simon Greenwood, Adam Barnes, Tory Gordon-Harris and Antonia Bolingbroke-Kent

Cover artwork Patricia Fraser

Cover design Tory Gordon-Harris

Maps supplied by CollinsBartholomew a subsidiary of HarperCollins*Publishers* Ltd. Reproduced by Permission of HarperCollins Publishers.

Production Jo Ekin

Printing Colorcraft, Hong Kong

UK Distribution Portfolio, London

USA and Canada Cimino Publishing Group

Province intro photographs:

New Brunswick: Ross Mavis, Inn on the Cove
Quebec: Au Gré du Vent

All other incidental photographs courtesy of the Canadian Tourism Commission.

Contents

Acknowledgements
Explanation of Symbols
Introduction
Maps

Symbols
and what they mean

 No credit cards accepted

 Meals can be provided, often by prior arrangement

 Rooms all have TVs

 Children are welcome without proviso

 Working farm

 Off-street car parking

 Access only for wheelchairs

 Full wheelchair facilities

 Swimming available in pool, sea, dam or river

 Good hiking or walking direct from the house

 They have their own horses for riding

 No-smoking inside the buildings

Introduction

GREENWOOD GUIDES APPROACH

If I could be allowed to draw a mining analogy then we, the hard-working, stamina-rich Greenwood Guides inspection team, were diamond diggers with a vast amount of rock and coal to blast and sift. Canada ain't small. No one ever said it was. Four of us drove in two-week bursts across this vast landmass, eastwards and westwards from our base in Toronto (I won't claim we went south to north!), in quest of those rare places to stay where we felt uplifted by our visit. Spurred on by dreams of Northern Lights, icebergs, maples and wolves, we drove and drove and then drove some more - almost 25,000 kilometres up hill, down dale, across plain and through six time zones.

Some stretches of road were exquisite, our hire cars tiny metal boxes glinting in giant landscapes: through the misty Rockies of Jasper National Park; along the northern shore of Lake Superior; around the Cabot Trail on Nova Scotia's Cape Breton Island; from ferry to ferry up BC's Pacific Coast. Our inner poets – usually quiet, rather self-conscious chaps, keen on limericks – were roused to Wordsworthian heights of passion and sensitivity.

Anyway… if we eventually chose a place for the book it was because we felt excited about the opportunity to write it up later. We probably could have done with the services of Wordsworth as an editor back at the office, but we have tried to describe each place with all the enthusiasm that we felt at the time of our visit. And also to avoid cliché, waffle and meaninglessness wherever possible!

We were always conscious of how much *you* would enjoy each place, treading confidently in our footsteps. We have been ruthlessly selective on your behalf. For every place we liked there were at least four that we didn't… and that is after exhaustive research, whittling down a jungle of possibilities. You can only imagine how many B&Bs, lodges, hotels etc there actually are in a country like Canada. 'OK' was never enough of an accolade and sometimes turning a place down was extremely hard because it so nearly fitted the bill.

There has been absolutely nothing written on Canadian accommodation until now that provides you with the skeleton of a great holiday rather than simply listing a thousand B&Bs in every town across the land and leaving you to take pot luck.

We have selected just 87 places. They are of amazing variety in terms of style, but they have one thing in common. They are run by people who by nature provide their guests with far more than the contractual minimum. Great accommodation is not defined by how much you pay and what you get for your money. It is a complex compound of atmosphere, place, creature comfort and human interaction. We gravitate towards places that have something I'm going to call 'soul', like it or not.

This is not a full-blown directory of accommodation therefore. You will often be disappointed if you expect to find a Greenwood place in a particular town. Not every town has great places to stay. The book is designed to be followed as a guide book. Stay in our places as destinations in themselves and meet lovely, warm, friendly, humorous Canadians. And experience not just B&Bs, but wilderness lodges, lighthouses, houseboats, ranches, farms, townhouses, self-catering options, even a couple of swish Quebec hotels. Only the character and humanity of each place determines its acceptability.

Our natural biases have often leant towards the lived-in feel, artistic inclination, creative design, historical interest… but only if these qualities are backed up by owners who have a real liking for other people and take a real pleasure in looking after them.

At its simplest the Greenwood Guides approach is to recommend places that we have been to ourselves and particularly liked.

EXPENSIVE DOES NOT MEAN GOOD

There are essentially two types of place to stay. There are those that fulfil their obligations in a commercial way and leave you feeling throughout your stay like the paying customer that you are. And there are those few great places where you feel welcomed in and treated as a friend, cliché though this may now have become, and where paying at the end of your visit is a pleasurable surprise. It is a strange irony in the accommodation world that no price is ever put on the essential qualities of a place – people, atmosphere, charm. These terms are too woolly, perhaps, to quantify, but this is where one's real enjoyment of a place to stay stems from. You are asked to pay instead for tangible facilities like marble bathrooms and en-suite showers.

This is a fallacy that we try to dismantle in all our guides, which is why you will find places at all price levels. Expensive does not mean good. And nor does cheap, however appealing the word may sound! If a place costs plenty then it will probably offer facilities in keeping with the price. But that does not mean you will have any fun. Some very expensive places forget that they are providing a service and look down their noses at their own guests. At the other end of the spectrum, the very cheapest places are often cheap for good reasons. Sometimes for truly excellent reasons!

Character and genuine hospitality, the extra qualities we search for, are found spaced evenly across the price spectrum. The places to stay in this guide range from $70 – $500 per couple per night. Nowhere cuts corners at the risk of your displeasure. We give equal billing to each place we choose, no matter if it is a gorgeous lodge or a home-spun B&B.

At the top end, the most jewel-encrusted, nay 'boutique' (a word that has snuck into accommodation vocab somewhere along the line!) places may drip with luxurious trimmings, but have retained their sense of atmosphere and humour, are friendly and informal, and nearly all are still family-owned and -run.

Equally there are places in the book that do not have much in the way of luxury, but easily compensate with unique settings (lighthouses and boats for example), wonderful views and charming hosts.

It is the quality of experience that draws us in and this is not determined by how much you pay.

In the end I know that you will really like the owners in this book, many of whom we now count as friends. And you will certainly make friends yourselves if you stick to the Greenwood trail.

WHEN TO GO
At the risk of stating the achingly obvious, travelling out-of-season will allow you greater freedom to arrange your itinerary and make last-minute bookings. You should, however, be aware that some establishments close completely from October/November to April/May – this information can be found on each property's entry page. If no mention is made of the property's opening times, then it is open all year round.

DRIVING
Canadian roads are generally excellent. Some suffer winter frost damage and so have a slightly uneven surface, but this is never a problem. Extra care is

required on the unsurfaced roads, which stretch out through parts of the countryside.

If hiring a car, you should consider the 'unlimited mileage' packages. The standard allowances of 150 to 200 km per day do not go very far in rural Canada, and your holiday could be soured by annoying extras on your bill. One-way rentals (picking the car up at A and dropping off at B) may also incur hefty charges, and if you are booking these yourself you should shop around.

Should you be driving in winter and there is a chance that you will encounter snow, it's worth getting snow tyres. For rental cars, the extra charge is around $10 a day, but if there is snow on the road, these tyres are worth their weight in plutonium: rather than slither around and get stuck in petrol station forecourts, you will enjoy some much-needed traction. I speak from experience, believe me! Getting hold of them is invariably harder than it sounds, because while you usually book your car through a central system, the snow tyres are allocated locally. When booking, ask for the number of the office from which you will actually take the car and ring them separately to ensure they will have a snow-tyred car for you.

Speed limits vary from province to province, and at the upper end they are either 100km/h or 90km/h – signs keep you well informed. These are enforced quite rigorously, and the Greenwood Guides have unfortunately not been shy of adding to the Highway Patrol's coffers. The same applies to parking in the cities. Do not underestimate the traffic wardens. Park in the wrong place and you WILL get a ticket. Ask the B&B owners for advice.

MOOSE
The roads of (parts of) rural Canada are lined with signs warning of these creatures. They are enormoose and have a habit, which defies all Darwinian survival theories, of lumbering onto roads at dawn, dusk, and sometimes in-between. Keep an eye out.

DIRECTIONS
We have provided directions, unless a 30-word spiel was unlikely to clarify matters. Most owners can fax detailed maps/directions or tell you a web site that can help. Remember, once more, that distances are big. In Canada-speak, "Turn left at the next Stop sign" could indicate a 20-kilometre drive.

RECOMMENDATIONS FOR JUST A FEW EATERIES THAT WE PARTICULARLY LIKED:
By the Way Café, 400 Bloor St West, Toronto, tel: 416-967-4295 for

atmospheric lunches.

Sushi on Bloor, 515 Bloor Street West, Toronto, tel: 416-516-3456.

Jacques Bistro du Parc, 126A Cumberland St, Toronto, tel: 416-961-1893.

Ted's Range Road Diner, R.R.#1, Conc. 9, Range Road, Meaford, ON, tel: 519-538-1788.

Common Loaf Bakery, 180 First St, Tofino, BC, tel: 250-725-3915.

Café Brio, 944 Fort St, Victoria, BC, tel: 1-866-270-5461.

Restaurant Temps des Cérises, 79 du Carmel, Danville, QC, 1-800-839-2818…

…and that's all you get. There must have been others to tell the truth, we seemed to eat out quite a lot. But we prefer to allow the owners in the book to advise, with far more up-to-date expertise, on where to eat and what to do when you get there. We concentrate solely on accommodation in this guide.

PAY FOR ENTRY

We could not afford to research and publish this guide in the way we do without the financial support of those we feature. Each place that we have chosen has paid an entry fee for which we make no apology. It has not influenced our decision-making about who is right or wrong for the guide and we turn down many more than we accept. The proof of this is in the proverbial pudding. Use the book and see for yourself. It is also very hard for us to write up a place that we are not enthusiastic about.

TAXES

In Canada, provincial and national sales taxes – totalling between 7 and 15 per cent - are almost never included in the price quoted for goods and services. Most places in this book have to charge tax on their accommodation, apart from those smaller establishments whose annual income falls below a certain threshold. Some of the tax you do pay will be refundable for non-Canadians on leaving the country. But it is fairly complicated what is refundable and what is not. And it often depends on which province you are in. Tax on accommodation is on the whole reclaimable, but restaurant meals are not. Keep individual receipts worth $50 or more. The total receipt value must exceed $200 to make a claim.

Given that tax varies from province to province, that some places might have to start charging, and that some visitors can reclaim it, we have quoted all prices EXCLUSIVE of tax, as is the norm in Canada. In 95 per cent of places, you'll have to pay it when you settle your bill. If necessary, ask when booking. Tax is a bit of a minefield (there's a surprise) and if it is of importance to you, you should make your own enquiries to the Canadian authorities to get more detail. Sorry not to be more help!

PRICES AND PAYMENT
Prices are quoted in Canadian dollars per couple sharing per night, unless specifically stated otherwise. Single rates are also given. We have provided a range to allow for expected price increases over two years. There might be unexpected increases if the property changes radically or exchange rates alter, in which case we would ask you to be understanding.

Quite a few places do not accept payment with credit cards – these have a 'CASH' symbol in the book – but may take travellers cheques or other forms of payment. Again, ask when booking.

MONEY
At the time of writing, the exchange rate was £1 = CAN$2.50.

TIPPING
In restaurants, taxis, hairdressers, it is normal to tip around 15 per cent of the bill.

There is no need to tip petrol pump attendants who fill up your car. In B&Bs, there is no hard-and-fast rule, but tipping is not generally expected.

MAPS
The maps in this book are not road maps, but merely indicators of where the properties are. You should get a detailed road map when you arrive.

CANCELLATION
Cancellation policies vary as much as the wallpaper and should be clarified on booking. Many establishments will ask for a credit card number when you book so that they are not wholly compromised if you fail to turn up.

SMOKING
Not indoors you won't.

TELEPHONES
Canadian toll-free numbers are not free if dialled from outside North America. The owners are generous, not foolhardy. If you do call a toll-free number from outside North America, a message tells you that you have to pay.

When in Canada: if the call is local, you only need dial the last seven numbers. For other calls within North America, dial 1 followed by the ten-digit number. If dialling internationally (apart from to the US), key 011 followed by the international code.

Calling Canada from abroad: the international dialling code is 1. So to call Canada from Britain, you key 00 1 then the ten-digit phone number. If calling a toll-free 1-800 number from Britain, you would dial 00 1 800 etc.

LANGUAGE
Canada has two official languages, English and French. Outside Quebec, the country is very anglophone, while Quebec itself is very francophone. Montreal is a bilingual city, although traditionally the eastern side is French-speaking and the western English-speaking. Elsewhere in the province, most of those involved in tourism speak some English, but you will deal with people who do not. You don't need to speak French to enjoy Quebec, but with a smattering you will get more out of the experience.

THANKSGIVING
Is in mid-October in Canada, not November.

DISCLAIMER
We make no claims to god-like objectivity in assessing what is or is not special about the places we feature. They are there because we like them. Our opinions and tastes are mortal and ours alone. We have done our utmost to get the facts right, but apologize for any mistakes that may have slipped through the net. Some things change which are outside our control: people sell up, prices increase, exchange rates fluctuate, unfortunate extensions are added, marriages break up and even acts of God can rain down destruction. We would be grateful to be told about any errors or changes, however great or small. We can always make these editions on the web version of this book.

PLEASE WRITE TO US
Our email address is editor@greenwoodguides.com for all comments. We are always grateful to hear how much/little you enjoyed the places in the book.

We also have guides to Australia, New Zealand (second editions due at the end of 2003) and South Africa (now in second edition, third edition due in May 2004). These books are available in bookshops or by emailing us direct.

Our web site address is www.greenwoodguides.com.

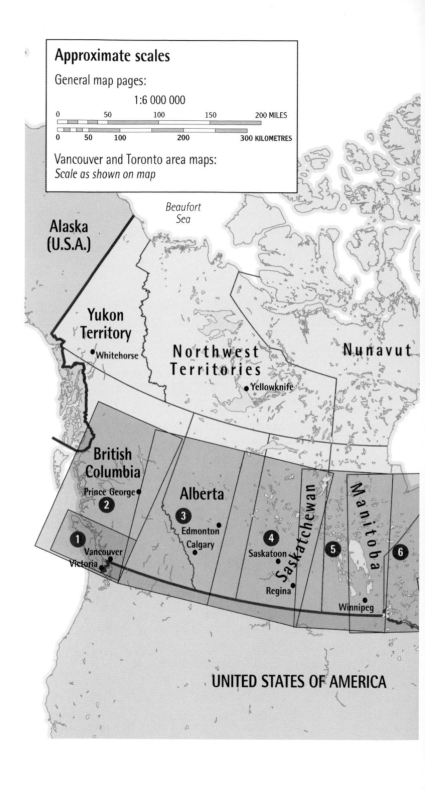

Approximate scales

General map pages:

1:6 000 000

| 0 | 50 | 100 | 150 | 200 MILES |

| 0 | 50 | 100 | 200 | 300 KILOMETRES |

Vancouver and Toronto area maps:
Scale as shown on map

Alaska
(U.S.A.)

Beaufort
Sea

Yukon
Territory
● Whitehorse

Northwest
Territories
● Yellowknife

Nunavut

British
Columbia
Prince George ●
2

Alberta
3
● Edmonton
● Calgary

Saskatchewan

Manitoba

Saskatoon ●
4

● Regina

5

6

1
Vancouver ●
Victoria ●

Winnipeg ●

UNITED STATES OF AMERICA

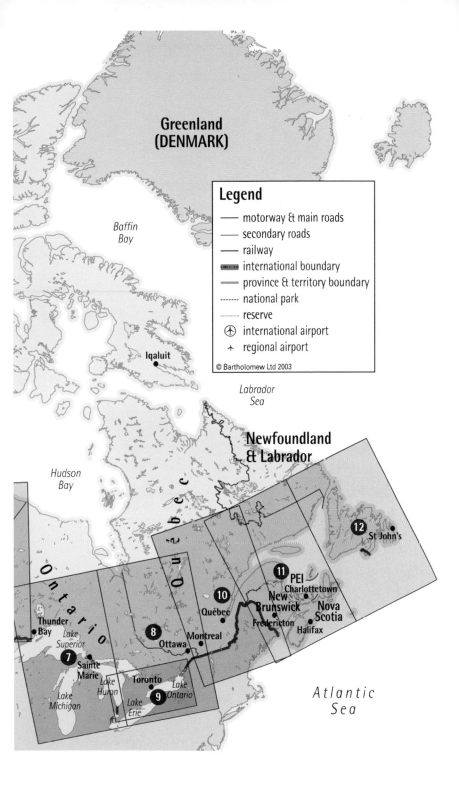

Greenland
(DENMARK)

Baffin
Bay

Legend

— motorway & main roads
— secondary roads
— railway
▬▬ international boundary
— province & territory boundary
------ national park
.... reserve
✈ international airport
✈ regional airport

© Bartholomew Ltd 2003

Iqaluit

Labrador
Sea

Newfoundland
& Labrador

Hudson
Bay

Québec

Ontario

12 St John's

11 PEI
Charlottetown
10
Québec
New
Brunswick
Nova
Scotia
Fredericton
Halifax

Thunder
Bay
Lake
Superior
8
Ottawa
Montreal

7
Sainte
Marie

Lake
Huron
Toronto
Lake
Michigan
Lake
Erie
9
Lake
Ontario

Atlantic
Sea

VANCOUVER ISLAND

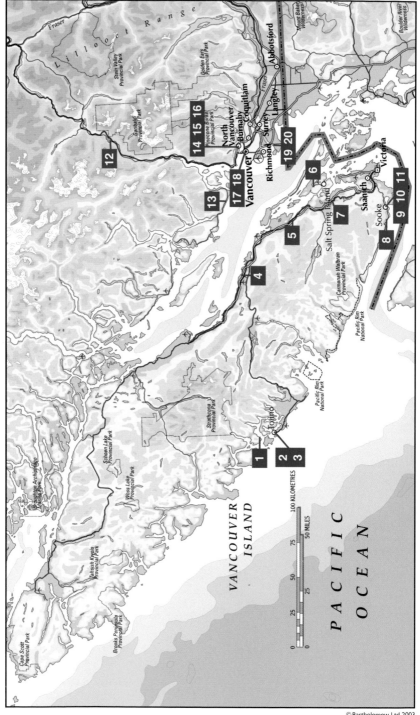

Map 1

© Bartholomew Ltd 2003

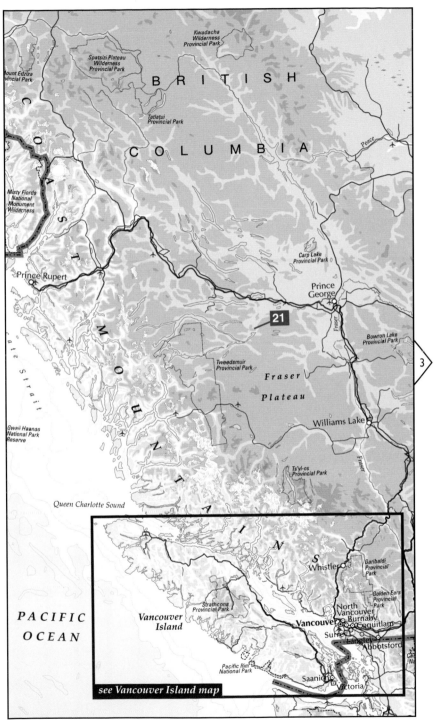

B R I T I S H

C O L U M B I A

Kwadacha
Wilderness
Provincial Park

Spatsizi Plateau
Wilderness
Provincial Park

Mount Edziza
Provincial Park

Tatlatui
Provincial Park

Peace

C O A S T

Misty Fiords
National
Monument
Wilderness

Carp Lake
Provincial Park

Prince Rupert

Prince
George

21

Fraser

Bowron Lake
Provincial Park

Tweedsmuir
Provincial Park

Fraser
Plateau

3

M O U N T A I N

Strait

Gwaii Haanas
National Park
Reserve

Williams Lake

Ts'yl-os
Provincial Park

Fraser

Queen Charlotte Sound

PACIFIC
OCEAN

Vancouver
Island

Strathcona
Provincial Park

Whistler

Garibaldi
Provincial
Park

Golden Ears
Provincial
Park

North
Vancouver   Burnaby

Vancouver   Coquitlam

Surrey
Langley

Abbotsford

Pacific Rim
National Park

Saanich
Victoria

see Vancouver Island map

Map 2

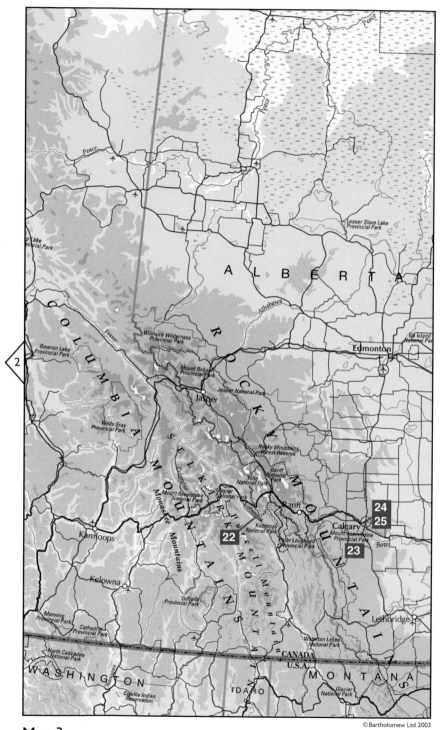

Map 3

© Bartholomew Ltd 2003

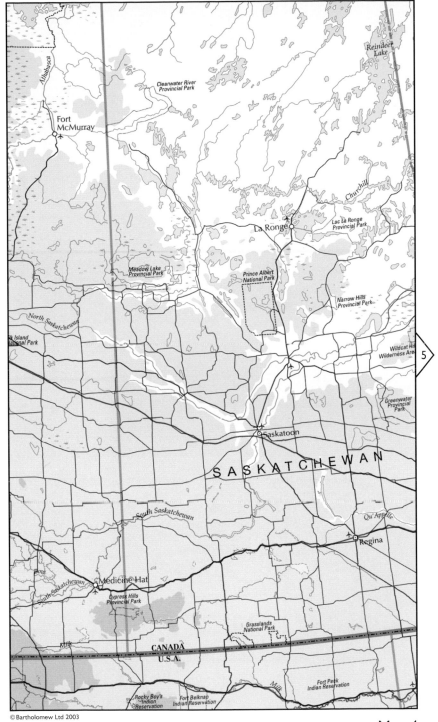

Map 4

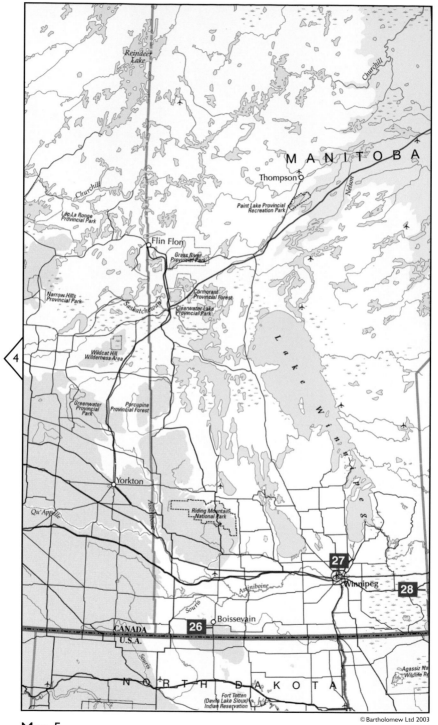

Map 5

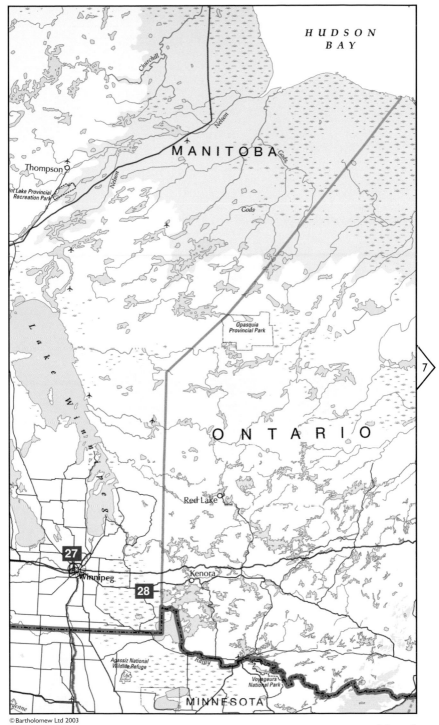

Map 6

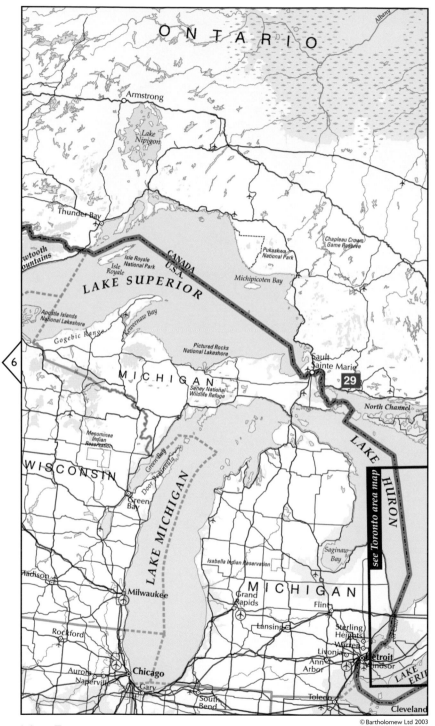

Map 7

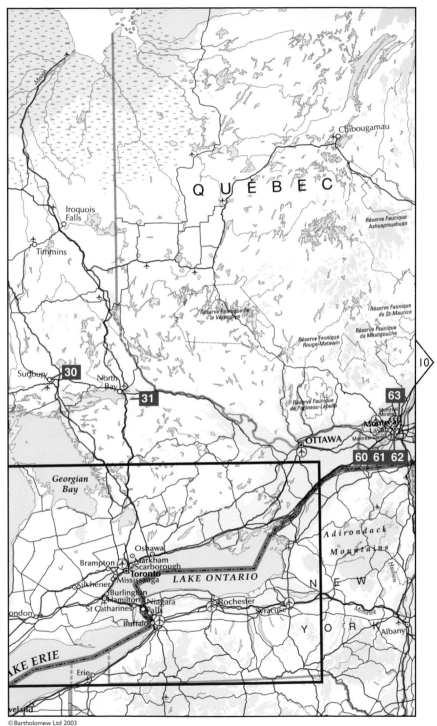

© Bartholomew Ltd 2003

Map 8

TORONTO AREA

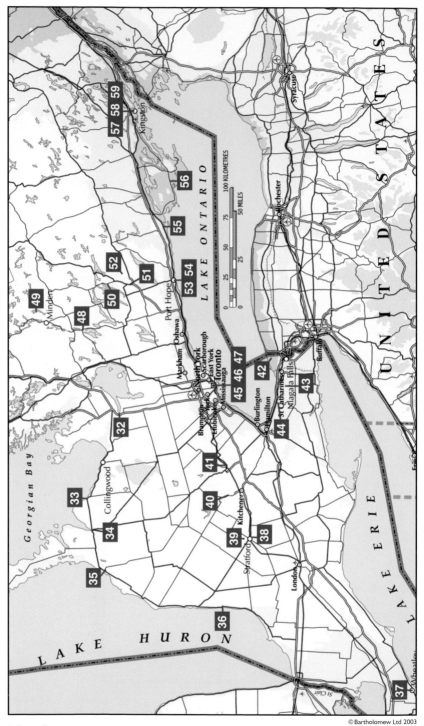

Map 9

© Bartholomew Ltd 2003

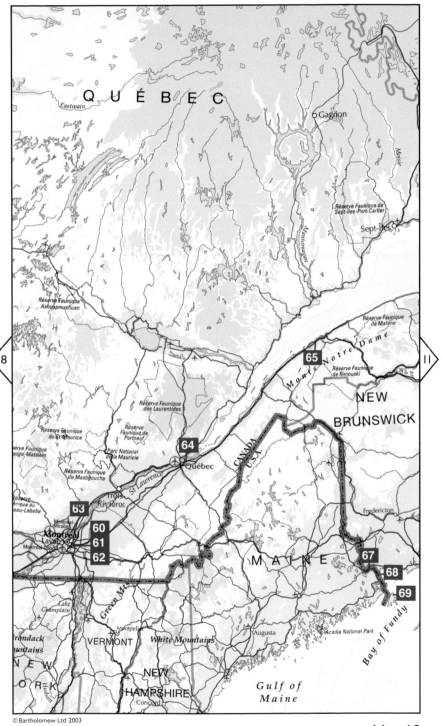

Map 10

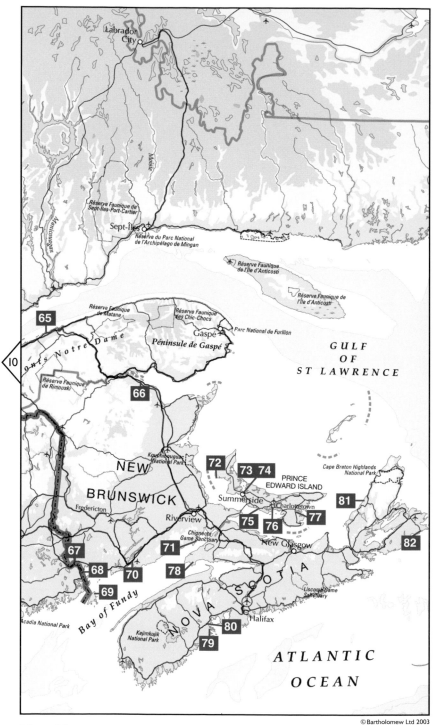

Map 11

© Bartholomew Ltd 2003

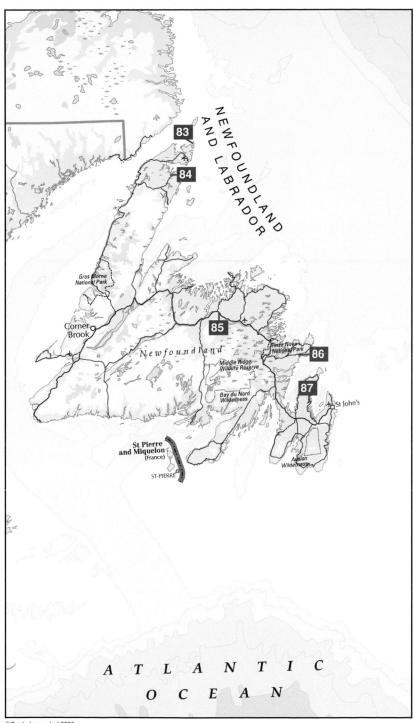

NEWFOUNDLAND AND LABRADOR

Gros Morne
National Park

Corner
Brook

Newfoundland

Middle Ridge
Wildlife Reserve

Terra Nova
National Park

Bay du Nord
Wilderness

St John's

St Pierre
and Miquelon
(France)

ST-PIERRE

Avalon
Wilderness

83
84
85
86
87

A T L A N T I C

O C E A N

Map 12

British Columbia

The Innchanter

Shaun Shelongosky
Hot Springs Cove, Tofino V0R 2Z0
Tel: 250-670-1149
Web: www.innchanter.com
Cell: 604-219-3494

There's a first time for everything...or a few things in this case. Hot springs, sea-planes and midnight walks through the rainforest, not to mention sleeping in the underbelly of a magnificent 86-foot wooden ship. Everything about The Innchanter is exciting, adventurous and at times verging on the riotous. The charismatic Shaun is both a master of informality and a culinary wizard – hence plentiful feasting and merriment in a fantastically casual atmosphere. Within ten minutes of arriving six of us were diving into a fondue and cracking open the wine, elbows everywhere, noisy banter being flung around; not your typical B&B scene. After dinner (and after breakfast) entertainment was a trip to the hot springs, playground and shower of The Innchanter. A winding boardwalk through the shadowy rainforest leads you to the Pacific Ocean where a steaming 104-degree waterfall pours three metres into a series of pools, a romantic paradise for late-night star-gazing. Edible delights herald your return, and the cosy beamed sitting room with its roaring fire and extensive library is just the spot to unwind. Bedrooms are simple and characterful; art on the walls and the Captain's Quarters still houses the old ship's wheel. Shaun calls it 'glorified camping' but methinks camping never knew such glories. A laugh-a-minute and a personal favourite. *Ask for transportation details from Tofino. Kayaks and rowing-boats available.*

Rooms: 7: 5 doubles and 2 singles sharing 3 bathrooms.
Price: $98 per person bed, breakfast and dinner. Captain's Cabin slightly more.
Meals: Full breakfast and dinner included. Shaun is chef.
Directions: 28 km north of Tofino by tour boat or float plane.
Postal Address: PO Box 99, Lions Bay, BC, V0N 2E0.

British Columbia

Middle Beach Lodge

Jeff Hale

PO Box 100, Tofino V0R 2Z0
Tel: 250-725-2900 Fax: 250-725-2901
Email: lodge@middlebeach.com Web: www.middlebeach.com

At Middle Beach you are just going to have to reduce the revs of your normal life. Surf, wilderness, majesty of nature, that's what it's all about here in the wild west. And the lodge is the perfect place to drink it all in. Its position, on a headland, which jags like a finger into the Pacific between Mackenzie and Middle Beaches, is spectacular. The mighty Pacific surrounds you, and at night the crashing waves fill your senses. Waking up with the sweeping expanse of Mackenzie Beach and the endless aquamarine ocean literally on my doorstep was a truly invigorating experience. Here Nature dictates and the structure of the various buildings at the Lodge is organic, designed with the preservation of the environment in mind. The timber is largely recycled from old warehouses in Victoria, and the beautiful teak doors you'll see throughout were originally built in 1925 for a P&O liner. Middle Beach is divided between two lodges (one designated adult-oriented, the other more family) and the cabins. The bedrooms are rustic, chic and a world away from frilly Victoriana. Jacuzzis and private hot tubs are the norm. The main lodge is where eating takes place and the vast beams, squishy sofas and gigantic fireplace of the Great Room make it a great place to hang out. Middle Beach is a place for all seasons… rain or shine, the majesty of the West Coast refreshes the soul. *Hiking, kayaking, surfing, bicycling, whale-watching, golf.*

Rooms: 64: lodge suites (kitchen, fire, king bed, jacuzzi); lodge rooms (bath/shower); self-contained oceanfront cabins (kitchenettes, fireplaces and hot tubs).
Price: $90 – $395. Group retreats welcome. Ask about prices.
Meals: Continental breakfast included. Dinner in summer 7 nights a week. Off-season 2 nights a week. Seafood buffet $31.50 pp.
Directions: From Tofino head out of town towards Ucluelet. Middle Beach Lodge is on the right after about 5 km.
Closed: Over Christmas, 17th - 26th December.

Map Number: 1

The Inn at Tough City

Ron Gauld and Johanna Vander Kley
350 Main Street, PO Box 8, Tofino V0R 2Z0
Tel: 250-725-2021; toll-free 1-877-725-2021 Fax: 250-725-2088
Email: cityinn@alberni.net Web: www.toughcity.com

A whippety figure in a dashing fedora bounded up the stairs to greet me… so this was 'Crazy' Ron! Tales of this Tofino legend had pre-empted my visit and the rumours are true, he is crazy – in the best possible way – and seems to operate at about three times the speed of the rest of us. I'll have what he's having. The inn, on Tofino's waterfront, mirrors this energy and humour. Never a dull moment here. The colours hit you as soon as you enter the hallway, antique advertising signs advertising more quirkiness within. The rooms are similarly vibrant. Every one is painted a bright hue and psychedelic stained glass transforms bathrooms into prisms of colour. Aeroplanes hang off the ceiling in one room, a totem pole sits solemnly in the next and beautiful hand-carved whale doors lead onto the balcony in another. Even the brickwork and railings have a story – the bricks were recycled from Gastown in Vancouver and the balcony railings started life in 1880s Austria. Ron is particularly proud of his 'cool beyond cool' antique Japanese tin toys in the Sushi restaurant, and the comical giant Buddha salvaged from a 1950s San Francisco Chinese restaurant. A feast for the eyes and a fistful of merriment. Tough City was the colourful original nickname of Tofino, by the way.

Rooms: 8: 2 twins, 1 king and 5 queens. All have en-suite bath/shower, balconies, cable TV and phone.
Price: $75 – $190. No single rates.
Meals: No breakfast. Summer restaurant open for lunch and dinner. Winter dinner from 5 pm onwards.
Directions: Go into Tofino on the only road, turn right on Second Street and you'll come to the inn on Main Street, which runs along the Tofino waterfront.

Blue Willow Guest House

John and Arlene England
524 Quatna Road, Qualicum Beach V9K 1B4
Tel: 250-752-9052 Fax: 250-752-9039
Email: bluewillow@shaw.ca
Web: www.bluewillow.bc.ca

Blue Willow is straight out of a storybook, the sort of place you might expect to run into hobbits or Alice (of Wonderland fame) or Mrs Tiggy-Winkle. Everything about it is, well, sweet. The garden is divine, like a mini Garden of Eden where romantic nooks are hidden amid the profusion of plants. A white hydrangea clusters over the door and blue-edged windows peer out from beneath leafy mantles. Plants definitely have the upper hand, and the cottage seems to do gentle battle with a sea of rambling flora. There's probably some fauna in there too. Inside, the house is equally adorable. Arlene's devotion to British *House and Garden* is patent and you'll have to remind yourself you're in Canada, not a cosy Suffolk cottage. John, a dashing ex-NATO fighter pilot, dons his apron and serves an exotic breakfast in the snug beamed sitting room while Arlene chatters away and generally spoils you. An array of silver and of course the Blue Willow china add to the occasion. My room was brimming with character and the dinky turquoise claw-foot tub persuaded me to indulge in a second bath of the day. Fresh flowers are always in abundance. *For those after a little more seclusion, there is the garden cottage.*

Rooms: 3: 1 twin/king with en-suite bath/shower; 1 queen with en-suite bath/shower; 1 cottage with 1 queen, 1 double and 1 single, bath and shower.
Price: $100 – $140 double occ. Single occ. $85 – $100.
Meals: Full breakfast included.
Directions: From Hwy 19 take exit 60, direction Qualicum Beach. Through town to the waterfront (Hwy 19a). Turn right and take first right after the Heritage Inn sign (Hall Rd). Quatna is first left and 524 is near the end on the right-hand side.

Yellow Point Lodge

Richard and Sandi Hill

3700 Yellow Point Road, Ladysmith V0R 2E0
Tel: 250-245-7422 Fax: 250-245-7411
Web: www.yellowpointlodge.com

This island institution instils the kind of loyalty in its guests normally reserved for the National Hockey League. My neighbour at dinner, Margarite, had been coming since 1943 and enthused about the 'extended family'; another couple, who were married here 60 years ago, had been back every year since to celebrate their anniversary. It even has its own fan club, *The Friends of Yellow Point Society!*, devoted as much to the Hill family as to the lodge. Richard's remarkable father Gerry bought the 165 acres in the early '30s, having had his eye on the property since childhood. Long before it became fashionable Gerry wanted a place committed to the preservation of the environment, where people could immerse themselves in nature. Seventy years on, his son Richard remains true to this vision. You won't find a TV here, but at this 'summer camp for grown-ups' you'll find an abundance of other entertainments – the problem is choosing which one. I opted for lounging in the magnificent 'hanging-out room' with its endless sofas, huge fireplace and vast beams. And then there's the food. Three enormous, tasty meals are enjoyed communally, and the table is never empty of some tempting treat. This is a casual, fun place, perfect for any season. Go off-season, mid-week and you'll be flabbergasted at the good value. *Hiking, tennis, kayaking, bicycling, massages, boat trips all on offer.*

Rooms: 58: a mix of lodge rooms, cabins and cottages.
Price: $119 – $194 for double occupancy. $66 – $122 for single occ.
Meals: All meals included.
Directions: From Highway 19 going south take Cedar Rd (left) before Ladysmith. At Husky petrol station go right onto Yellow Point Rd. About 5 miles further on you will see Yellow Point Lodge on right-hand side.

Beddis House B&B

Terry and Bev Bolton

131 Miles Avenue, Salt Spring Island V8K 2E1
Tel: 250-537-1028; toll-free 1-866-537-1028
Email: beddis@saltspring.com Web: www.beddishousebandb.com

As migrants from Calgary via Venezuela, Norway and England, Terry and Bev are still blessing the 'piece of serendipity' that brought them here. Salt Spring is a magical place, and the Boltons have landed on a special slice of it. The location is prime, with its own little beach and crystal clear waters right at the end of the garden. Apparently the scuba-diving is great – I took their word for it and stuck to the hammock. Deer are regular visitors; several were unabashedly munching apples when I was there. The green-fingered Boltons aren't quite as pleased to see them as their guests are. The orchards and gardens have an unmistakable English flavour, probably something to do with their creators. English immigrants the Beddises were one of the first families on the island, and built the house in 1900. That's positively ante-diluvian in Salt Spring terms. The Coach House, a more recent addition, is where the rooms are. Each has a different flavour, my favourite being the 'Gingham' room, intentionally evocative of a farmhouse. Blues and yellows give it a cheery feel, while the claw-foot tub adds a further touch of rusticity. Breakfast in the sunny dining room is 'quite a serious affair', as is afternoon tea. These B&Bs really are the enemy of the waistline. You could of course go hiking, but don't forget to be back in time for tea.

Rooms: 3: 1 queen, 1 king and 1 twin/king; all with en-suite bath/shower.
Price: $150 – $200 for double occ. Singles $135 – $185.
Meals: Full breakfast and afternoon tea included.
Directions: South from Ganges. Left onto Beddis after Seabreeze Inn. 6 km along, turn left onto Miles Ave and Beddis House is ahead of you.
Closed: Mid-Nov - mid-Feb.

Fairburn Farm

Anthea and Darrel Archer
3310 Jackson Road, Duncan V9L 6N7
Tel: 250-746-4637 Fax: 250-746-4637
Email: info@fairburnfarm.bc.ca Web: www.fairburnfarm.bc.ca

It was on one of those golden late autumn days of preternatural clarity that I drove up the 'No Through Road' to Fairburn Farm. Unravelling myself from the car, I took a few minutes just breathing in the magical view across the Koksilah Ridge: a sea of trees shimmering away to the horizon, and not a sound to disturb the bright morning air. I loved it already. But the best was yet to come, for Anthea and Darrel are the proud owners of the only herd of River Water Buffalo in North America. Coming face to face with these noble beasts (and their excellent hairstyles) is a great experience. With 29 animals at present, plans are afoot to set up a dairy. Soon you'll be spooning buffalo yoghurt over your granola. Fairburn Farm has always been a pioneering kind of place. Darrel's parents bought it in 1955 and started the first organic co-op in Canada; the same philosophy persists today. Vegetables, herbs and grains are all home-grown and Anthea even grinds her own grain for bread. This is a true retreat. Endless forest and pasture surround you and a beautiful creek winds lazily along the bottom of the ridge. The farm bedrooms are comfortable and there is the cottage for those wanting extra seclusion. Disappointment will only arise if you stay a night, not a week. *Fabulous walking.*

Rooms: 3: all queens: 1 with en-suite bath/shower, 2 with jacuzzi baths. Cottage sleeps up to 7 with full kitchen and bathroom.
Price: $135 – $150 double occupancy. Singles from $115 – $130. Cottage $850 per week.
Meals: Full breakfast included. Can do dinner by arrangement for about $20 a head.
Directions: Go south over silver bridge in Duncan. At second lights after bridge right on Allenby Rd. 2nd left on Koksilah. Right onto Jackson Rd after a few kilometres. Follow to end of road.
Closed: October 1st - April 1st.

French Beach Retreats

Harry and Sissel Hammer
983 Seaside Drive, PO Box 98, Sooke V0S 1N0
Tel: 250-642-5250; toll-free 1-866-522-5250
Email: info@frenchbeachretreats.com Web: www.frenchbeachretreats.com

An eerie mist curled round the trees as I drove down the track to French Beach. Ahead of me the sun was dipping down behind the distant mountains, crowning them with a fiery halo and throwing a kaleidoscope of colours across the darkening sky. Remote, wild and infinitely romantic, French Beach is just a little further up the coast road than Sooke, and well worth the few extra kilometres. The situation is superb and a few evenings of sunsets like that will do wonders for any high blood pressure. The main house is right on the cliffs, trees sheltering you on one side while on the other the cliffs plunge away to the ocean below. Everything has been designed with nature in mind. Giant windows frame the ever-changing natural cinema, binoculars await passing wildlife and the wide wraparound deck juts so temptingly over the ocean you could almost dive off into the blue (you'd have to be very brave indeed though!). I could spend hours on that deck just wallowing in the beauty of it all. Inside, a towering totem-pole watches over things and the open brick fireplace keeps chilly winter evenings at bay. For the more adventurous, the treehouse offers a slightly alternative experience. And don't forget to whistle while you walk – bears, wolves and cougars also live here! *On San Juan Hiking Trail. Beside beautiful French Beach.*

Rooms: Main house: 2 queens and 1 bunk queen sharing 2 bathrooms (jacuzzi/shower/bath/sauna); Treehouse: queen en/s bath/shower.
Price: $125 – $295 double occ. $25 an extra person. $750 – $1700 a week.
Meals: Continental breakfast included.
Directions: Follow Hwy 1 and then 14 out of Victoria. Drive straight through Sooke and follow West Coast Rd (Hwy 14) until Woodhaven, about 25 km. Follow Woodhaven to the end and turn right onto Seaside Drive.

Richview House

François and Joan Gething

7031 Richview Drive, Sooke V0S 1N0
Tel: 250-642-5520; toll-free 1-866-276-2480 Fax: 250-642-5501
Email: richview@bnbsooke.com Web: www.bnbsooke.com

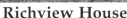

If François and Joan were smug then they would have every right to be! Those wicked Ontario winters they escaped from 34 years ago seem a universe away as we chat in the fall sunshine. The Pacific is so close you could use the lawn as a diving board, and across the straits of Juan de Fuca the sublime Olympic Mountains loom majestically. I instantly thought of lazy summer days drinking Pimms and playing croquet, perhaps being distracted as the odd bald eagle glides by. François is one of those amazing men who built most of the house and its contents in about a week and thinks nothing of it. As we wander round, Joan casually points out his handiwork; yellow cedar and fir beds, Douglas fir floors, the dining-room table and the awesome wooden-framed aromatherapy shower for two. It would take pages to list it all. Bright splashes of South American art on the walls add vibrancy to the calming, minimalist rooms and everyone has the luxury of a private hot tub. Vast windows maximise the stunning views; you don't even have to get vertical in the morning to gaze at the ocean. Joan's breakfast is quite an affair. You won't get a fry-up, but fruit-filled crêpes, caramelised nut bread and an array of deliciousnesses (if that's a word) are far more exciting options. Felix, the gorgeous Hungarian vizla, can always help you walk it off.

Rooms: 3: 2 queens with en-suite bath/shower; 1 queen has steam shower for 2. All 3 have outdoor hot tubs.
Price: $150 – $225. No single rates.
Meals: Full breakfast included.
Directions:: Through Sooke (from Victoria direction). Past traffic lights, turn left down Whiffen Spit Rd (big B&B signs). Richview Drive at end on right. Their house is very soon on the left.

Map Number: 1

The Lighthouse Retreat

Virginia Boyd

107 West Coast Road, Sooke V0S 1N0
Tel: 250-646-2345; toll-free 1-888-805-4448 Fax: 250-646-2345
Email: info@lighthouseretreat.ca Web: www.lighthouseretreat.ca
Cell: 250-216-1356

More treehouse than lighthouse, this is a place to ignite the fires of creativity in your soul. The whole place seems to hang over the ocean, and as you walk down to the maze-like structure you'll begin to get that excited feeling in the pit of your stomach. Totem poles greet you as you descend, hinting at the artistry within. And the ocean glints and scintillates ahead of you. Rooms are dotted about the retreat, from the 'Aviary' room, protruding in 360-degree glass splendour from a wooden platform, to the cottage and the main house. All have spectacular views and their mix of vibrant art, white walls and floods of sunlight make them fresh and energising. Meanwhile the bathrooms are pure innovation. Mine was a blue stuccoed cavern with a giant pod-like shower; next door an amazing mosaic climbed the walls – one of your host's artistic ventures. Being a feisty redhead she claims such projects keep her out of mischief. And oh-my are the beds comfortable, and so large I felt like the princess without the proverbial pea. The lighthouse concierge can arrange numerous services and indulgences for you, even a chef and a singing butler! There are many options for relaxing; spend a while in 'Jamaica' (AKA the sauna), amble down to the beach, do some yoga, soak in the hot tub. This place is truly outstanding.

Rooms: Rented as a whole: 7 or 8 rooms, 2 kings, 8 queens and 4 singles. All have private bathrooms, mostly with jacuzzis. Sleeps up to 24 people.
Price: Per week: $5000 – $8500.
Meals: Self-catering. A chef can be provided at about $120 – $150 a day.
Directions: Go through Sooke towards Port Renfrew (north). Lighthouse Retreat is 14 km past stop sign in Sooke, at top of a hill on the left.

Map Number: 1

Sooke Harbour House

Sinclair and Frédérique Philip

1528 Whiffen Spit Road, Sooke V0S 1N0
Tel: 250-642-3421; toll-free 1-800-889-9688 Fax: 250-642-6988
Email: info@sookeharbourhouse.com Web: www.sookeharbourhouse.com

Hallelujah!, I thought, lost in gustatory rapture, I love my job. As course after delectable course was delivered with relish, I succumbed wholly to the spell of the Sooke Harbour House. With its reputation sprinting before it, the place had a lot to live up to. Tales of the artwork, a 14,450-bottle wine cellar, infamous edible gardens and sensational food had set the picture… and I wasn't disappointed. I doubt anyone ever is. Beauty and talent abound here and Sinclair and Frédérique's passion for what they do pervades everything, their inspiration still the life-blood after 23 years at the helm. Inside, a gallery of local talent adorns every surface (including the elevator), while outside the two acres of gardens tumble down to the ocean in a festival of scents and colours, their contents all being groomed for the dinner plate. Everything eaten here is organic, seasonal and local; the latter to the extent that olive oil is eschewed and replaced by locally pressed nut and seed oils. Culinary wonders aside, the rooms are artistic and luxurious. My *Passionflower* room – its namesake trailing over the window – had a bath you could do lengths in while admiring the ocean, and a bed *de luxe*. As I sat on my lush private verandah at breakfast, contemplating the Olympic Mountains emerging through mist in the distance, I decided that the rumours were definitely true. A very special place indeed.

Rooms: 28: all with ocean view, kings or queens, local art, private deck patio, en-suite bathroom and fireplace.
Price: $280 – $555. No single rates.
Meals: Breakfast is included. Packed lunches are complimentary in summer. Dinner by reservation $75 a head without wine.
Directions:: From Victoria take Hwy 14 to Sooke. Thru' Sooke, past 2 stop lights. About 1 km on you will see big blue 'lodging' sign saying Sooke Harbour House. Turn left down Whiffen Spit Rd. Inn at the end on the right.

Edgewater Lodge

Jay Symons

8841 Highway 99, PO Box 369, Whistler V0N 1B0
Tel: 604-932-0688; toll-free 1-888-870-9065 Fax: 604-932-0686
Email: jays@direct.ca Web: www.edgewater-lodge.com

The Symons family have owned this estate since 1965. Sitting in the widest part of the Whistler valley, it wasn't until 1995 that the envisaged lodge beside Green Lake was built. Long and low, the building was designed so that every bedroom has a view of the lake and the mountains. And what a view it is! The windows are veritable walls of glass – fall asleep to the twinkling lights of the remote handful of houses across the lake, and wake to broad valley vistas and views of Wedge Mountain, Armchair Glacier and, of course, Whistler and Blackcomb. It's a mere 15-minute cross-country ski to the resort of Whistler (these mountain types are hardy folk). Hiking, skiing, walking, kayaking, canoeing, biking, snowshoeing, windsurfing, rollerblading and even water-skiing are all available. But if soaking in a lakeside jacuzzi or reading in a swing-seat is more your speed, then Edgewater can also accommodate. Either way, just make sure you are ready for a big supper. The bar and restaurant with vaulted ceilings and head-turning views serves the intriguing "chef's rambles" and other serious morsels; venison with herb béarnaise, seared Camembert and fig mousse. As Jay says, Edgewater is a great escape from the "just-add-water-and-stir" commercialism of Whistler proper.

Rooms: 12: 6 with en-suite bath, 6 with en-suite shower, sitting area and their own balcony.
Price: $105 – $320 double occ.
Meals: Better-than-Continental breakfast included (home-made granola, yoghurt, fruit salad, croissants, cinnamon buns etc). There is a dining room for dinner.
Directions: North of Whistler on Highway 99 for about 5 km, sign on right-hand side to Edgewater Lodge. Follow signs down drive.

Map Number: 1

Country Cottage B&B

Philip and Loragene Gaulin
1183 Roberts Creek Road, PO Box 183, Roberts Creek V0N 2W0
Tel: 604-885-7448

Of all the lovely places to be found along the Sunshine Coast, the little village of Roberts Creek stands alone. As much for its Liliputian quaintness, with its library and restaurants, as for its one outstanding place to stay: Loragene and Philip's Country Cottage Bed and Breakfast, two private cottages on their two-acre farm. Cedar Lodge is "a tree-house for grown-ups". A stairway up to a deck negotiates the 90-year-old red cedar and leads you into a large converted barn. Furniture by the "twig people", Mexican throws, First Nation art and fishing-hunting-skiing accoutrements all live happily side by side. A writing desk groans under books, and sofas and rockers huddle around a stone fireplace. Then there's Rose Cottage, smaller, even cosier, just as delectably rustic with a big iron bed, old pine dresser and hearty log-burner. Loragene is a sparkling hostess, quick to laughter. She chops the wood, feeds the chickens, the Romney ewes and two enormous Irish wolfhounds, Ceilidh and Seamus – your dogs are welcome! Complimentary bones! And she brings a wonderful breakfast to your cottage door, including her trademark "Eggs Lorageneadict", all ingeniously cooked on a 1927 wood-burning stove. There are also toys for boys. Philip's 'thing' is cars – a Dodge Truck folly in the field, another in the garage along with a Ferrari and a BMW bike. Something for everyone – stay as long as you can!

Rooms: 2 cottages: Rose Cottage has 1 queen with en-suite bath; Cedar Lodge has 2 queens sharing 2 bathrooms.
Price: $85 – $145 for single or double occupancy.
Meals: Full breakfast included. Tea and scones in the afternoons.
Directions: Take the ferry from Horseshoe Bay to Langdale. Follow 101 (Sunshine Coast Highway) then left onto Roberts Creek Rd into Roberts Creek, house on right.

Map Number: 1

British Columbia

Thistledown House

Ruth Crameri and Rex Davidson

3910 Capilano Rd, North Vancouver V7R 4J2
Tel: 604-986-7173; toll-free 1-888-633-7173 Fax: 604-980-2939
Email: davidson@helix.net Web: www.thistle-down.com

Rex has owned and run two restaurants in Vancouver and Ruth takes food as seriously as her passion for design and architecture, so you can be sure that your tummy is in good hands (so to speak). Treats to which you just *cain't* say no are put out for tea and left by the bedside, and unusual and very wonderful breakfasts spring forth like rabbits from a hat: fennel croustadine with wild fiddlehead greens, fillets of trout with sea asparagus and lovage marinade for example. They look fabulous and taste better, and Ruth somehow manages to find time for a chat too.... *and* she has her own interior design practice. The house is traditional and, not surprisingly, very stylish and comfortable, with masses of room in which to be sociable or to sit quietly, either under the apple tree in the garden, in the sunroom, or by the fire in the sitting room. You will, however, have to share the run of the place with two Scottish terriers, Talla and Tosh. There is a theme here; with an English mother and a Scottish father, Rex is rather fond of a certain island across the pond – and Ruth was born in Switzerland which might account for her natural facility with languages.

Rooms: 5: all queens and kings with en-suite bath.
Price: $110 – $250 for double occupancy. Singles $95 – $220.
Meals: Full breakfast included.
Directions: On Capilano Rd about halfway up on the right.
Closed: Whole of January recovering from Hogmanay.

Map Number: 1

Mountainside Manor

Anne and Mike Murphy

5909 Nancy Greene Way, North Vancouver V7R 4W6
Tel: 604-990-9772; toll-free 1-800-967-1319 Fax: 604-985-8470
Email: mtnside@attglobal.net
Web: www.vancouver-bc.com/mountainsidemanor

The highest, most aptly named and probably most stylish house at Grouse Mountain, Mountainside Manor has a view of jaw-dropping splendour and an interior to match. Lions Gate Bridge pokes out of the morning mist, alongside the treetops and skyscrapers of Stanley Park and downtown Vancouver. The vista is truly breathtaking and helps explain why Mike and Anne bought this house 12 years ago directly from the architects' blueprint. It is made entirely of cedar and glass, and inside, a curved staircase rises up from the large hall and climbs an interior wall partially constructed of glass tiles. All is light, bright and ultra-modern. Every room has its own bathroom and vast windows to make the most of that view. Outside, the bird filled garden has decking, hot tub and a multitude of shrubs, which drift seamlessly into the wilderness of the mountain behind. The energetic can work up an appetite for breakfast with the 'Grouse Grind' an hour of vertical walking – but there is a cable car for the more self-indulgent. Mountainside Manor provides the perfect combination of city and wilderness: you're just ten minutes from Vancouver's centre yet can regularly see deer. *Anne and Mike also have some very central self-catering apartments in Whistler.*

Rooms: 4: 3 with en-suite bathrooms and 1 with private bathroom across the hall.
Price: $95 – $175. No single rates.
Meals: Full breakfast included.
Directions: Head up Capilano Rd towards Grouse Mountain. Mountainside Manor is the last house on the left-hand side.

Laburnum Cottage B&B

Delphine Masterton

1388 Terrace Avenue, North Vancouver V7R 1B4
Tel: 604-988-4877; toll-free 1-888-207-8901 Fax: 604-988-4877
Email: laburnum@shaw.ca Web: www.laburnumcottage.ca

Delphine is a celebrated local character, who grabs life with both hands. She drives a gold convertible, loves to gas, has been on the telly, and thinks nothing of trekking in Nepal aged 56. She makes Laburnum Cottage a required stop on her own. With five children and 11 grandchildren, she is used to comings and goings, entertaining, guests… a real 'multi-tasker' as modern idiom would have it. The B&B was just an extension of all the things she naturally did anyway. And she has gathered together a great little team to help her. Chef Karin spoils you rotten with a magnificent three-course breakfast, and a gardener maintains the award-winning beds and borders of this rose-filled (very) English garden. Surrounded by virgin forest, a mountain stream trickles past the door of a secluded wisteria-wound summerhouse. Both Summerhouse Cottage and the Carriage House are private and pampering places to stay, although the flower-inspired bedrooms in the main house are equally charming: old-style prints, Liberty fabrics and fine English antiques inherited from her mother fill the bedrooms and the house. Tea and shortcake (or sherry in the evenings) are taken in the sitting room, or when warming hands and feet by the Aga in the kitchen. A romantic and restful homely house. *Swimming, horse-riding, hiking, boating, mountain-biking and great restaurants available in the area.*

Rooms: 6: both cottages have TV, baths and fireplaces. All rooms have private bathroom. Carriage House has queen and loft with double for kids.
Price: $125 – $250 double occupancy. Retreat and long-stay specials.
Meals: Full breakfast included.
Directions: Lions Gate Bridge, North Vancouver exit to Marine Drive. 1st light left on Capilano, about 1 mile to Paisley. Follow the Murdo Fraser sign, continue right on Phillip to Terrace Ave. Number 1388 is on a corner at the bottom of the hill.

English Bay Inn

Boban Vuckovic and Greg Wald

1968 Comox St, Vancouver
V6G 1R4
Tel: 604-683-8002;
toll-free 1-866-683-8002
Fax: 604-683-8089
Email:
stay@englishbayinn.com
Web: www.englishbayinn.com

Even just stepping off the lively, bustling downtown streets, strewn with high-rise buildings, into the small and traditional English Bay Inn is quite an experience. The sitting room with lavish candelabras, Persian rug, French antiques, classical music, ticking clocks and a crackling fire sets the tone. Collections of books and CDs are there for you to choose and use. Boban is a self-confessed "crazy European" and the owner of the inn. You are likely to encounter him over a glass of wine or a game of chess. He says he always wins (which sounds like a challenge for someone). Perhaps that's why he puts the decanters of port and sherry in the bedrooms. There are chocolates there too. The muted country-house colours, exposed brick walls, mahogany furniture and feather beds are in cahoots, and make you seriously consider lengthening your stay. Greg, the manager, runs the inn super-smoothly, and is greatly entertaining at breakfast. He cooks it himself and particularly applauseworthy are the freshly-baked scones, bursting with fruit. A big foodie and long-term local, he can point you in the right direction for all the best, hidden, West End eating spots and watering-holes.

Rooms: 5: 4 rooms with en-suite bath/shower;
1 room with en-suite shower; all queens.
Price: $170 – $330. Singles on application.
Meals: Full breakfast included.
Directions: In Downtown Vancouver at crossroads of Comox St and Denman St. Head north towards Stanley Park. English Bay Inn is on the left-hand side.

Graeme's House

Graeme Webster
2735 Waterloo Street,
Vancouver V6R 3J1
Tel: 604-732-1488;
toll-free 1-888-732-6660
Fax: 604-926-7046
Email: graeweb@telus.net
Web:
www.graemewebster.com

As I walked up the street my instincts told me I was heading somewhere special. A decrepit old bicycle, now colourfully draped from seat to pedal in flowers, indicated that I had arrived at my destination... but I couldn't see the actual house for plants. I had to look quite closely to find the path leading to the front door. Graeme welcomed me into her living room where comfy chairs and heaps of books and magazines encourage you to sit around the fireplace and read. But the magnetic heart of this homely 1920s cottage is the kitchen and with the best will in the world that's where you'll end up too: yellow, breezy, light-filled, and stuffed with family bits and bobs, portraits, paintings and collections of glassware. Large double doors are flung open onto a roof terrace, where you can sit and have breakfast in a shady spot and pick apples from the upper boughs of the apple tree that grows in the back garden below. Like the front garden, it's crammed with mirrors and seats, tables and baskets, pots and plants and colour. Ferns, red acacia, azaleas, begonias, maple – anything that grows, including me, seems to like it here. Two of the bedrooms have private little balconies, and the Rosedale room and new Lighthouse suite have treetop views. All are filled with quirky antiques and commissioned stained glass. Unpretentious and wonderful.

Rooms: 1 queen and 1 twin sharing bathroom and separate washroom; 1 suite with queen and en-suite bath; 1 queen with en-suite shower.
Price: $90 – $165 double occupancy. $80 – $115 for singles.
Meals: Continental breakfast included (excellent fresh-baked muffins, fruit salad, toast etc).
Directions: Kitsilano District of Vancouver on Broadway, take a right onto Waterloo. She's number 2735.

Duck Inn Riverfront Cottages

Jill and Allen York
4349 River Road West, Ladner V4K 1R9
Tel: 604-946-7521 Fax: 604-946-7521
Email: duckinn@dccnet.com Web: www.duckinn.net

In describing this float home on the delta of the Fraser River it's going to be hard not to mention the ducks. Anything 'duck' goes, from coat-stands and notepaper, to bed linen and wallpaper. Returning guests add to their numbers. One couple spent their anniversary (!?) counting and came up with over 800. However, by the time you read this, some may well have migrated south to the new Water Garden cottage downstairs. Why? Closer to the river, a private hot tub? Who knows what motivates a duck? Probably Jill. She runs this place with obvious enjoyment and (can I say?) flamboyant attention to detail, off-the-wall and otherwise. The floating Florida room, for example, with its hot tub, fairy lights in the shape of flamingos, and climbing plants growing madly in all directions is a favourite place for absorbing local information from that weighty tome 'Duck Inn Details'. This covers everything, including ghosts. Sherry, sketchbooks, robes and slippers, boats and bicycles are all supplied. Lok-style smoked salmon, from Allen's smokehouse, along with cream cheese, capers and bagels are packed in the fridge. Fabulous restaurants, a bird reserve and long riverside walks are local Ladner attractions. But more convenient and harder to beat is the pleasure of dangling one's toes in the water from a private dock, supping a local tipple, and watching the wildlife drift by.

Rooms: 2 cottages/suites. Both have full bathroom with bath/shower.
Price: $100 – $180 for double occupancy.
Meals: Self-catering but a full fridge of goodies is provided. They smoke their own salmon by the way.
Directions:: Ladner is half an hour south of downtown Vancouver. Take Highway 99 south through the George Massey tunnel, staying in the right lane. Take exit 29, turn right on Ladner trunk road which becomes River Road West.

River Run Cottages

Barb and Will Watkins

4551 River Road West, Ladner V4K 1R9
Tel: 604-946-7778 Fax: 604-940-1970
Email: info@riverruncottages.com Web: www.riverruncottages.com

Although all four cottages are delightfully romantic, it's the bathroom that swung the pendulum of my favour-detector towards the Waterlily. Set in the shower wall of this delightful two-level floating cottage is a goldfish tank – filled with weed and tiddly-wee electric blue fish. Watery and nautical, this little cottage feels like a boat – lots of wood, an upstairs loft bed, and windows reminiscent of a ship's bridge, through which one can look out onto the to-ing and fro-ing of sailboats, fishing boats, swans and geese. Binoculars are provided. All four cottages have their own distinct charms. The Netloft has a private Japanese soaker tub outside, and the Keeper's Quarters has a large waterside deck. Over a bridge, the Northwest Room, with a four-poster log bed, has a slate and stone bathroom with double-head shower that makes showering like stepping into a waterfall. All have CD players, wood-burning fireplaces, private decks and barbeques. On arrival at this tranquil place, fresh-baked goodies are waiting for you, and a scrumptious breakfast is delivered to your door with the morning paper. Which leaves you in peace to get on with the serious task of enjoying yourself. *Bicycles and kayaks are available for guests. Ask about children.*

Rooms: 4 cottages: all queens with en-suite bathrooms; 1 with jacuzzi/shower; 1 with tub on deck and shower; 1 with grotto double-head shower; 1 bath/shower.
Price: $130 – $210. Less $10 for single occupancy.
Meals: Full 2-course breakfast included. Romantic catered dinners can be arranged. Call for prices.
Directions: Heading south on Highway 17 take right turn onto 10 (Ladner trunk road). Carry on for 2 miles till it turns onto River Rd West.

Nechako Lodge & Aviation

Josef and Elisabeth Doerig

PO Box 2413, Vanderhoof V0J 3A0
Tel: 250-690-7740; toll-free 1-800-567-7022 Fax: 250-690-7740
Email: nelo@uniserve.com Web: www.rainbowtroutfishing.com

The Kenney Dam has created the Nechako lake system, the spindly fingers of which stretch through the Tweedsmuir Provincial Park and to the distant Coast Mountains. The lodge sits on the easterly Knewstubb Lake in a secluded bay near the dam. Foolhardy types have been known to take a five-week trip, and canoe or kayak the watery loop, but it seems to me preferable, and exciting, to charter Josef's float plane, strap a canoe to the side (I'm not joking), get dumped in the wilderness (not too far), and make your way back home. The two boys are qualified guides and canoe instructors (if you need them), and are immensely capable. They built the little cabin that sits on the lakeside, with logs hauled from the lake and cut by hand – aged just ten and twelve. They are also keen fishermen. Rods can be hired, and you can tie your own flies, or at least try; all the kit is there. The accommodation is basic, but with all the important essentials, comfortable beds, lots of hot water and large log fires. Elk and monstrous moose horns adorn the walls in the sitting room, seriously squidgy leather chairs and piles of National Geographic provide a pleasurable hour before dinner. Four courses of great Swiss food (also breakfast and packed lunches) are all cooked by Elisabeth and ensure that you stay full of beans (energy that is).

Rooms: 9: 5 rooms in the lodge each with three beds sharing 2 showers; 2 large cabins indoor washroom and shower; 2 small cabins use of a showerhouse.
Price: $110 – $125 double occupancy. Singles $83 – $115.
Meals: Full breakfast included but any combination of meal options possible. Cabins are self-catering but you can order any meal as an extra. Flexibility rules!
Directions: 2.5 hours in total from Prince George. Head west on Highway 16 till Vanderhoof. Take road on left hand side to Kenney Dam. From there follow the Nechako Lodge signs. Last 1 hour on gravel road.
Closed: Nov - April. Opens 1st May.

Wells Landing B&B

Ron and Jan van Vugt
4040 Sanborn Road, PO Box 89, Parson V0A 1L0
Tel: 250-348-2273; toll-free 1-877-912-9022 Fax: 250-348-2008
Email: info@experiencetherockies.com
Web: www.experiencetherockies.com

A large sign points you off the highway to cross over to the other side of the Columbia Valley, the largest wetland habitat in North America. Lying between the Rockies and the Purcell Mountains, it's your personal playground when you stay at Wells Landing. The new log house stands on the river bank and is guarded by Zeus, a huge, hairy Bernese Mountain Guide Dog and Belgian Shepherd cocktail, who is on the payroll as protector (from predators) and friend of all... ably assisted by his tiny sidekick Sparky. Inside, your awe will be inspired, in no particular order, by the space, the design, the woodworking, the hi-fi system, the enormous windows, the staggering view, the quiet, the wilderness and the welcomes. And once settled in your room (ask for the room with the "loo with a view") you can then get down to the business of exploring. The original log house that Ron and Jan fell in love with, and lived in for four years while deciding what they wanted to build, still stands on the property, albeit slightly lopsidedly. Greenhouses and flower gardens nurture the surprises that await you at breakfast. Trails have been cut through the forest, for walking or skiing. There are canoes, kayaks, bikes, a hot tub, and even a teepee. I fell asleep star-gazing over the mountains where eagles and osprey nest – and I swear I heard the clattering of a moose on the pebbly spit below my window.

Rooms: 3: 1 king with en-suite bath; 2 kings with en-suite shower.
Price: $75 – $125.
Meals: Full breakfast included.
Directions: Highway 95 heading south from Golden for 35 km. At the sign take a right at Parson River Crossing Road. Over five single-lane wood bridges that cross the Columbia River and Wetlands. Left at Sanborn Rd. Continue until you can go no further – 3 km.

Alberta

Homeplace Ranch

Jayne and Mac MaKenny

Site 2, Box 6, RR 1, Priddis T0L 1W0
Tel: 403-931-3245; toll-free 1-877-931-3245 Fax: 403-931-3245
Email: mac@homeplaceranch.com Web: www.homeplaceranch.com

An overnight dump of November snow had turned my car into a gibbering wreck (I was fine, of course) so I reverted to plan B. Having left the main road, the hour-long walk to the ranch was magical. The track winds between birches and firs, past horses and cattle. All is wonderfully peaceful – not bad, considering Calgary is little more than half-an-hour away. Mac, Jayne and Jessi are lords and ladies of all they survey. Mac was a rodeo-rider in his youth, but earns his thrills less dangerously these days. He runs this 7,000-acre ranch in the foothills of the Rockies, and people return year after year, which says a lot about the surroundings and even more about the MaKennys. The emphasis, as you might expect, is firmly on horses. You're assigned a mount when you arrive and that's *yours* for the duration. With Mac and his cowboy helpers, you'll spend the days riding trails, checking the cattle… or you can opt out and just relax back at base. In winter, these activities stop and there is snow-shoeing or cross-country skiing instead. At this time of year you self-cater in the Coach House, but in horse season (May – late Oct) there are snug rooms in the lodge, which is where communal meals are served. If you want to discover your inner cowboy/girl, look no further.

Rooms: 8: 6 in lodge (4 upstairs, 2 down): 3 twin, 2 double/twin, 1 queen, all en-suite shower. 2 in Coach House: both queen, 1 en/s shower, 1 en/s bath/shower.
Price: From $683 pp (based on double occ.) for 4 days 3 nights. From $1179 pp for 7 days, 6 nights. Winter $600 per week for cabin for up to 6 people.
Meals: All inclusive, 3 meals and snacks. Everyone eats together. Horseback riding and ranch activities included in the price.
Directions: Homeplace is halfway between Priddis and Brag Creek on Highway 22. It is signposted off the road. Priddis is south-west of Calgary on Hwy 22.

Map Number: 3

Sweet Dreams & Scones

Karen McLeod
2443 Uxbridge Dr NW, Calgary T2N 3Z8
Tel: 403-289-7004 Fax: 403-289-7004
Email: karenbandb@hotmail.com Web: www.sweetdreamsandscones.com

Karen's Calgary home gives visitors a wonderful taster of old Canada. The house itself is modern and comfortable, never you fear, but it's rife with items that date from earlier times. I particularly loved the dining room, which showcases much of Karen's remarkable collection, including an array of irons, spindles and other kitchenalia. She is also a big fan of antique pine furniture; you can admire chunky double beds and dressers in some of the bedrooms, although my favourite sleeping quarter was the dark blue, rural-themed 'Simple Pleasures', with its sloped ceiling, wicker headboard and old farm implements. Karen's artistic talents do not just find their expression through collecting; her creative hand is everywhere. You can enjoy her hand-made wall quilts and willow chairs, and gaze longingly at her hats, bags and other winter accessories. Earthier needs will be met by home-baked breakfasts and specialities such as fruit-filled crêpes or decadent French toast, all served by the most important piece in the Sweet Dreams jigsaw, a vivacious hostess who charmed this Englander from the start. Garden enthusiasts, by the way, can enjoy a stunning display all spring, summer and early fall. *The house is very convenient for the Trans-Canada Highway and is only a short drive from downtown Calgary.*

Rooms: 3: 1 queen, 1 double and 1 with king and 2 twins; 2 en-suite bath/shower and 1 en-suite shower.
Price: $90 – $140 double occupancy. Singles $80 – $90. Two-room suite $160 – $180.
Meals: Full breakfast included.
Directions: Directions available on booking. 10 minutes to downtown.
Closed: Christmas week.

Calgary Westways Guest House

Jonathon Lloyd
216 25th Avenue SW,
Calgary T2S 0L1
Tel: 403-229-1758
Fax: 403-228-6265
Email:
calgary@westways.ab.ca
Web: www.westways.ab.ca/

This is a house that unashamedly bursts with colour, paintings, furniture and other such. Jonathon self-deprecatingly refers to this as "clutter" but he manages the trick of combining a homely atmosphere with everything you could need to feel pampered. When he moved to Canada from Merseyside in the early 90s, he only had a few ornaments with him, so Westways owes much of its diversity to the auction houses of Calgary. Walls are covered with paintings, newspapers, plates, photos. The pale green sitting room and dining room have their original bevelled windows, hardwood floors, large red rugs and lots of porcelain and glassware. The fun continues upstairs. I slept in a room called 'Rose' and hummed with contentment over the sitting room, entertainment system and soft gold bedspread. On the top floor are the two luxury suites. Both have wooden floors, large gas fireplaces and sumptuous beds, while 'Scollen' also boasts a jet-bath in the room and a balcony. Jonathon has trained as a chef so he's no slouch at breakfast either, and if you still can't quite persuade yourself to leave the house, the enclosed verandah with its under-floor heating is a great place for coffee. *Westways is very central to all Calgary's downtown shenanigans; there's public transport nearby, restaurants within easy walking distance, and a small park at the back of the house.*

Rooms: 5: 3 queen and 2 kings; all en suite, 1 with shower, 3 with bath/shower and 1 with jacuzzi and separate shower.
Price: $69 – $149 for double occ. Singles $59 – $129. During Calgary Stampede prices increase by $20 per room on summer prices.
Meals: Full breakfast included. 'Romantic Escape' dinners for 2 available by prior demand.
Directions: Available when booking.

Map Number: 3

Manitoba

Walkinshaw Place

Peter and Linda Albrecht

PO Box 833, Boissevain R0K 0E0
Tel: 204-534-6979; toll-free 1-888-739-2579 Fax: 204-534-3245
Email: walkinshawplace@mts.net Web: www.walkinshawplace.net

When Peter and Linda wanted to add 'B&B owners' to their résumés, they decided, as many do, to restore an old property. But rather than leave their Manitoba farm and move themselves, they simply found the house of their dreams and moved *it*. Snails around the world applauded. A large 97-year-old house 30 km from their farm caught their eye, so they transported it on the back of a gargantuan truck, settled it on some wooded land, spent six months on the restoration – it had been uninhabited for 24 years – and, *voilà*, a B&B was born. The gabled house, with its two-storey verandah, stands on a small rise on their 640-acre grain and beef-cattle farm, surrounded by trees and fields. It has a simple, country feel; pale walls and beautiful old fir floors are prevalent, with antique wooden furniture and lively quilts playing a supporting role. Modern contrivances such as air-conditioning and a hot tub keep you happily in the 21st century. The Albrechts live about three minutes away from this country retreat and, as locals born and bred, are awash with knowledge about the area and its particular attractions. *Turtle Mountain Provincial Park and the International Peace Garden are very near and you can hike, bird-watch, skate, or snow-shoe there, depending on the time of year.*

Rooms: 4: 3 queens and room with 1 double and 2 twins. Sofa beds available. All have en-suite bath/shower.
Price: $75 – $85 double occ. Singles less $15. Extra person $15 – $30.
Meals: Continental breakfast included. In summer you can BBQ your own steak on open fire. Package provided by local store for $15 pp.
Directions: 15 km south of Boissevain just off Highway 10, signed to your right.

River Gate Inn

Barry and Leslie Antonius
186 West Gate, Winnipeg R3C 2E1
Tel: 204-474-2761; toll-free 1-866-397-3345 Fax: 204-477-0664
Email: rivergate@shaw.ca Web: www.rivergateinn.com

This imposing, baronial house sits in Armstrong Point, an attractive area of Winnipeg where many prominent early townspeople built their homes. They would probably do the same nowadays. The Assiniboine River caresses the gardens, there are parks, restaurants and historical buildings within easy reach and, for a big city, all is surprisingly peaceful. River Gate stands out with its large roof with dormer windows, brick-and-wood façade and tidy lawns. Barry and Leslie spent two years acquiring furniture before they found a house suitable for holding it, and the combination – after a lot of work – is an immaculate sequence of carefully considered, vibrant rooms. The early 20th-century house was built along the lines of a 17th-century Scottish country home and the new colours match those available at that period. The hallway is mustard, the sitting room a pale cranberry, and the dining room a grassy green – nothing wishy-washy about this! A solid oak staircase takes you up to the bedrooms, although not before you've checked out the playground of a lower level with its entertainment systems and billiards table. There are two large-windowed, wooden-floored suites, one wheat-coloured, one blue, while the other rooms are smaller, but very comfortable. The friendly Antoniuses (Antonii??) allow guests their own space and this is a great place to relax around the pool in summer or round a large natural fireplace in winter.

Rooms: 4: 1 king, 2 queens and 1 double; all en suite, 2 with jacuzzi/showers, 1 bath/shower and 1 shower.
Price: $79 – $129 for double occupancy. Single occ. less $10. Discounts for longer stays.
Meals: Full breakfast included.
Directions: Available on booking or see web site www.rivergateinn.com.

Falcon Trails Resort

Rich and Lois Pettit and Barb Hamilton and Craig Christie
Box 130, Falcon Lake R0E 0N0
Tel: 204-349-8273
Email: relax@falcontrails.mb.ca Web: www.falcontrails.mb.ca

I awoke to the soothing sight of Falcon Lake stretching away beyond the wooded slopes that surround the resort. Had it been summer, I would have considered an early-morning canoe over to Picnic Island, but the late fall weather compelled me to slumber on. Falcon Trails is a small-scale wilderness-cum-ski-resort with 40 km of trails for hiking or biking, as well as canoeing and kayaking. In winter, you will be joined by some of the locals enjoying the 13 downhill runs, snowboarding park, tubing, cross-country skiing and snow-shoeing (that's with the tennis racquets) on offer. If that's not enough, you should also keep watch for the vast variety of local wildlife, which includes porcupine, bear, wolf, osprey, moose, marten, beaver and fisher. Guests self-cater in post-and-beam cabins with private beach or dock; all are modern constructions with pine in abundance, soaring ceilings, wood-burning stoves, decent kitchens, hot tubs (in most) and lake views. A particularly classy chalet style, you might call it. One-and-a-half miles away, two large, solar-powered cabins, with furniture hand-made by Craig, look over High Lake and enjoy a wonderful isolation. Lodge life is managed by the cheery Bill, who came to Falcon Trails as an unsuspecting guest and fell in love with the place, but the two couples that own the resort are intimately involved and all combine to put a very friendly face on a wilderness experience.

Rooms: 9 cabins: 8 have 2 queens and 1 single; 1 has just 2 queens; all have shower rooms.
Price: $139 – $175 for 1 or 2 people. Extra +$25, or +$10 if under 18. Weekly rates in summer $1250 for up to 4 adults; $119 for mid-week stays in off-season.
Meals: Self-catering.
Directions: Take Falcon Lake exit off the Trans-Canada Highway. After the stop sign take the right fork along South Shore Rd; a 15-minute drive brings you to Falcon Trails. Go to the office in the Welcome Centre.

Map Number: 5 & 6

Ontario

Bruce Bay Cottages and Lighthouse

Larry D. Peterson
PO Box 58, Bruce Mines P0R 1C0
Tel: 705-785-3473 (summer); 705-942-0416 (winter)
Fax: 705-785-3768 Email: larryd.peterson@sympatico.ca
Web: www.brucebaycottages.com

We British, with our piffling lakes and half-hearted storms, struggle with the concept of an inland lighthouse. Yet what would be a joke in the Lake District is a necessity on Lake Huron. The lighthouse is fascinating, a curiously squat affair on the tip of McKay Island, near the town of Bruce Mines, which was originally settled in the 1800s by Cornish miners. The lighthouse was rescued from destruction in the 1960s after the actual light had been moved to a nearby metal tower. The Peterson family built the causeways that connect McKay Island to the mainland via French Island. Since both islands are owned by the Petersons, guests can wander where they like. The interior of the lighthouse is not glamorous, but all essentials are provided, and the bedrooms, one of which used to be the battery room, are cosy. The view from the living area most certainly is glamorous, however, and people will often come in October to watch the lightning shows that vivify the autumn sky. Or in November to experience storms that have sunk many a Great Lakes ship. If you enjoy the wind in your hair, climb up a small ladder to the widow's walk, sing a shanty and look across the vast Georgian Bay. *On the shore-side of the lighthouse is a separate building, which is used for receptions throughout the year. The Petersons also have cottage accommodation on French Island.*

Rooms: 3: 2 doubles and 1 bunk and a convertible sofa (sleeps 6 altogether); all sharing 1 shower and 2 toilets. 1 group at a time only.
Price: $90 – $150 per day for the lighthouse.
Meals: Self-catering.
Directions: Entering Bruce Mines from the east you'll find Bruce Bay Rd towards the end of town on your left. Go down here, bear left and go over the bridge, then on to French Island and McKay Island.

Parker House Inn

Kathy and Michael Cull

259 Elm Street, Sudbury P3C 1V5
Tel: 705-674-2442; toll free 1-888-250-4453 Fax: 705-674-8573
Email: sudburyparkerhouse@on.aibn.com
Web: www.bbcanada.com/sudburyparkerhouse

A very relaxed, one-stop shop for those staying in Sudbury, Parker House has it all: central location, restaurant, on-site coffee roastery, cheery bar, fine accommodation and friendly hosts. The night I stayed the inn was full of people, local and not, and I really did hear more than one person mutter, "Ooh, this is nice," to their companions. I sat down in pale yellow surrounds, with salmon on the table and Louis Armstrong on the cornet, and chatted to Kathy about life in this part of the province. She has been in the hospitality business for a number of years, while Michael is a teacher with enough energy to run around helping at breakfast. Must be something in the water. The inn is just over four years old now, and has expanded into the house across the road, where there are three suites. That was where I slept, in a lovely room with wooden floors, rattan furniture and yellow-and-blue linen. Great bathroom too, with its wood floors, iron table and chairs. The rooms in the main house are smaller, but elegantly furnished, and coloured (and named) after some of the coffees that are made here. *The Culls also own a hand-hewn log cabin on a small lake 30 mins away.*

Rooms: 7: 5 queens and 2 doubles; all en suite, 5 with shower, 1 with jacuzzi and separate shower, and 1 with bath/shower.
Price: $75 – $150 for double occupancy. Single rates available.
Meals: Lunch and dinner à la carte. Continental breakfast included. Breakfast available to the public at weekends.
Directions: From Toronto follow Highway 69 north. Turn right on Paris St. Go 3 km then left on Elm (8th set of lights). Go through 4 lights, house is on left.

Hummingbird Hill B&B-Spa

Marianne and Gary Persia

254 Edmond Road, North Bay, (15 km south of North Bay) P0H 1K0
Tel: 705-752-4547; toll-free 1-800-661-4976 Fax: 705-752-5150
Email: mabb@vianet.on.ca Web: www.hummingbirdhill.ca
Cell: 705-495-5578

If "geodesic dome" is not part of your vocabulary when you arrive at Hummingbird Hill, then prepare for an education. Two conjoined domes provide an intriguing living space on the inside while the quirky exterior reminded me of the gingerbread house that lured Hansel and Gretel. The cedar-shingled home mixes sloping walls and surprising roof angles with windows where you don't expect them. Although it appears to be the work of an eccentric architect, chez Persia was actually built by a young couple who in 1973 set about imitating the work of American architect Buckminster Fuller. Bedrooms are furnished with antiques, wood-floored and cosy, and are reached by spiral staircases leading up from the timbered open-plan living area. The Loft Room has a particularly appealing bathroom downstairs with stove, sauna and bare brickwork, and you can lie in the bath watching deer feeding just outside the window. I awoke to a frosty fall morning – good for the soul, less beneficial for the pretty garden – and was sent on my way with a rousing breakfast and plans to return. The delights of the house should not blind you to Hummingbird Hill's other thrills. Many spa treatments are available, or you can spend your days canoeing, hiking, cross-country skiing, dog-sledding, horseback riding… come back for a massage, then sit down to supper. Fun, romance or both – all available on tap.

Rooms: 3: 1 queen with private bathroom with jacuzzi, separate shower and sauna; 2 doubles, 1 with en-suite bath/shower, 1 with en/s Victorian shower.
Price: $99 – $109 for double occupancy. Single occ. $85 – $95.
Meals: Full breakfast included. Dinner available by advance booking – you choose the style.
Directions: Off Highway 11 south, take Astorville exit and left onto Rd 654. Just past the Astorville Arena and Community Centre turn right onto Edmond Rd and Hummingbird Hill is 1.5 km on the right.

Richmond Manor

Pam and Bob Richmond
16 Blake Street, Barrie L4M 1J6
Tel: 705-726-7103
Email: richmond.manor@sympatico.ca
Web: www.bbcanada.com/1145.html

After 18 painstaking months of restoration Bob and Pam now have every reason to show off their large house in the middle of Barrie. Plumbing apart, they did just about all the work themselves, combining original features with their own creative input. Pam is an artist and her lovely designs are found throughout. The house, built in 1911, was designed in the 'great Georgian' style: brick, ivy, big windows and symmetrical proportions, a satisfying aesthetic combo which entranced the Richmonds from the moment they saw it. The 'For Sale' sign was just an added bonus! The house is near the road, and mere minutes to Barrie's beautiful waterfront and all the restaurants and shops thereabouts. Yet the house is entirely peaceful inside, and at the rear even backs onto a wood. The blue 'Williamsburg' bedroom is named after one of the Richmonds' favourite towns and is replete with designs from Virginia. The larger 'Lafayette' room has an unusual hunter green paint scheme. Bob the Doubter didn't originally believe it would work, but it does, and in spades. Trimmed in white, it has a four-poster bed and another beautiful design by Pam on the fire-guard. There's a TV room upstairs with myriad films, but you'll enjoy chatting with Bob and Pam in the light-filled sitting room if you are feeling sociable.

Rooms: 2: one queen, one double; shared bath/shower.
Price: $80 – $100 double occupancy. Singles $65 – $85.
Meals: Full breakfast included.
Directions: Leave Hwy 400 at exit 96 (to Dunlop St in Barrie) and follow the road to the east for 3 km where it turns into Blake St. The house is the first on the left, with the entrance up the side road to the left of the house.

Map Number: 9

Riverside Bed & Breakfast

Diane and Paul Ratcliff
157696 Concession 7, RR 2, Meaford N4L 1W6
Tel: 519-538-4376 Fax: 519-538-5462
Email: riversidebb@bmts.com Web: www.bbcanada.com/6582.html

Diane and Paul have finished their globe-trotting and started Riverside B&B, set in the heart of the beautiful Big Head River Valley. Lucky us. On July 1st the doors were opened, and they've already had people returning for more. Despite growing up in London (England not Ontario) Paul is a country boy at heart with a craving for open spaces. Fortunately for him Diane has similar tendencies, and with a mile of river and ten kilometres of trails on their doorstep there's enough here to amuse even the most ardent country bumpkin. The seasonal entertainment when I visited on a snowy December weekend was snow-shoeing, very exciting for a Brit in search of a quintessential Canadian experience. Warning – it's harder work than you think. But with Paul in his jazzy red outfit and (their retriever) Sydney's wagging tail leading the way, you know you're in good hands. When the ice recedes, there's great trout-fishing here and Paul's current record is a juicy 13-pounder. The house itself is an old farmhouse, replete with one of those magnificent old wooden barns that's not quite as upright as it was in its youth. The rooms are fresh and simple – think wooden floors and big squishy duvets – and breakfast is a wholesome feast, including home-made maple syrup. An English sense of humour comes free of charge. *Cross-country skiing, fishing, hiking. Downhill skiing 20 mins away.*

Rooms: 3: 1 twin with private bath/shower; 1 queen with en-suite shower; 1 queen with en-suite bath and shower.
Price: $85 – $95. $15 per additional person. $70 single in one room.
Meals: Full breakfast included.
Directions: If coming east along Hwy 26 towards Meaford, take Concession 7 (at tractor dealership). Right (south). They are 4.4 km down on right-hand side.

The Highland Manor

Paul Neville and Linda Bradford

867 4th Avenue 'A' West, Owen Sound N4K 6L5
Tel: 519-372-2699; toll-free 1-877-372-2699
Email: info@highlandmanor.ca Web: www.highlandmanor.ca

Majestically perched upon the Niagara Escarpment, this grand Victorian mansion is straight out of *Pride and Prejudice*. Enormous rooms with soaring ceilings are the perfect setting for marble fireplaces, grand pianos, ornate plaster mouldings and a smattering of antiques. The pianos, by the way, are not mere ornaments. Linda is a prodigious musical talent and she has played the piano to no less than four Canadian Prime Ministers. Photographs of her with various glitterati strew the surfaces. If you ask nicely you might get a private performance – but clearly this cannot be expected every day of the year. Long-standing Torontonians, the time came a few years ago for Paul and Linda to escape the Big Smoke and do what they'd always wanted, run a B&B. And 18 months on it's obvious to me that they're still loving their new vocation and get genuine pleasure out of making their guests happy. One newly-wed couple were reduced to tears by their efforts! The bedrooms are big and airy with painted or pine wooden floors and giant windows. With its fireplace and luxurious bed the *Fleming* got my vote, although the *Ross* has the bonus of a balcony. The gardens and wrap-around verandah, however, can be enjoyed by all. One for Victorian buffs. *Very near The Bruce Trail.*

Rooms: 4: 1 x 2 queens + double with en-suite bath/shower; 2 queens with en-suite bath/shower; 1 queen with shower only.
Price: $100 – $150 double occ. $80 – $100 singles.
Meals: Full breakfast included.
Directions: From Hwy 26 turn sth onto 9th Ave East. After 0.5 km at intersection (Esso on corner), R onto 10th St. Down hill, cross river, L onto 3rd Ave West (NOT East). After 1 block R on 9th St West. Up hill, see house on hill on L. Turn L, then L, then L again onto 4th Ave A West. House third from end.

Ontario

Chantry Breezes

Don and Jenny Amy

107 High St, PO Box 1576, Southampton N0H 2L0
Tel: 519-797-1818; toll-free 1-866-242-6879 Fax: 519-797-1862
Email: jenny@chantrybreezes.on.ca Web: www.chantrybreezes.on.ca

I immediately felt right at home here; off came the shoes, up went the feet and out with the book. Perhaps it was the particularly comfortable sofa or the cheery Christmas decorations, or the fact that Jodi had made me a great pot of tea. But I think it had more to do with Don and Jenny. Rarely do you meet a couple more committed to their guests' contentment. It is their apparent mission to fulfil all our little hearts' desires – as Roy Orbison once crooned, 'Anything you want, you got it.' Massages, yoga (Jenny's an instructor), dog-sledding, golf and romantic dinners are just a few of the things they'll happily arrange. Hammocks or sofas await the more horizontally inclined, but it's always nice to know you've got options. The Amys' other passion is Southampton – originally a childhood summer destination for them both – and their enthusiasm for the place is infectious. I had a great night's sleep snuggled under my cushy twill duvet, and thoroughly enjoyed both the Amys' company and Jenny's nutritious breakfast in the morning. Unfortunately the snow meant I couldn't sit in their jazzy green sunroom and taunt passers-by with the wafting aromas of freshly-baked muffins. Soul tonic. *2 mins to beach.*

Rooms: 6: 1 twin with en-suite shower; 1 queen and 2 singles en/s shower; 2 queens en/s shower; 1 queen en/s jacuzzi/shower; 1 double en/s bath/shower.

Price: $100 – $150 double occ. Singles $80 – $120. Ask for package options.

Meals: Full breakfast included. Caterer can be provided for private parties.

Directions: Follow Highway 21 to Southampton. At the stoplights, turn west on High St towards the lake. The B&B is located 2 blocks down High St on the left, at the corner of High and Huron Sts. Look for the white covered balcony.

Clair on the Square

Clair Soper

12 The Square, PO Box 158, Bayfield N0M 1G0
Tel: 519-565-2135 Fax: 519-565-5848
Web: www.claironthesquare.ca

You'd be hard pushed to find a more welcoming, ebullient hostess than Clair. The place feels less like a B&B and more like an extended summer lunch party where no-one's quite got round to going home. Contented guests lounge on the wooden deck or in the hammock, admire the rambling garden and come and go from the beach. But your hostess certainly isn't the only attraction. Built in 1857 as a farmhouse, the place has a casual-yet-chic feel, with chunky wooden furniture, gleaming wooden floors and local art. The garden-facing dining room is the centre of activity and you'll savour such delights as blueberry griddle cakes, fruit cobbler (personally tried and tested) and herb scones for breakfast. The three bedrooms are unfussy and luxurious. Beds are piled with cushions and you could be putting your belongings on an old washtub bench or in a Victorian bonnet dresser. Anyone with a penchant for poultry should opt for the chicken-tastic Rooster Room. And if you're really lucky you might get to see Clair serenading her disabled terrapin Hook, one of the inhabitants of the garden pond. *Bayfield is a delightful town located on Lake Huron and well worth several days.*

Rooms: 3: all queens; 2 with en-suite bathrooms, 1 with private; 2 with bath/shower, 1 with shower.
Price: $140 - $180 double occupancy. Single rates on request.
Meals: Full breakfast included.
Directions: Bayfield has a main square in the middle... and Clair is on the lake side.

Ontario

Wild Rose Guest House

Lily Shuster and Tom Hince
21298 Harbour Road, RR 1, Wheatley N0P 2P0
Tel: 519-825-9070 Fax: 519-825-9169
Email: peleetom@netcore.ca Web: www.netcore.ca/~peleetom

If you know your birds, or fancy joining the happy group that does, you really must spend some time in the teeming natural aviary of Wild Rose. The garden lies on a principal migratory route and Tom and Lily have spotted over 190 species, including 77 in one day! Tom would doubtless beat all-comers in naming them because he is the Discovery Channel's chief bird guru and has the enviable task of travelling the globe in search of the elusive greater-spotted magnolia-warbler. Lily accompanies him and combines these trips with minor haulage operations. Consequently, Wild Rose is strewn with exotica and you can sleep in rooms themed to the rainforest, the African savannah or – and I was persuaded to think this by the hand-painted Mexican sink – the south-west desert. Mexico was also the origin of the huge, rough-hewn, yellow pine dining table and chairs; birding certainly isn't the only attraction here. In May the couple arrange four-day packages where you'll discover the joys of both birding and Lily's culinary expertise. Expect to leave several pounds heavier! But even if you can't tell your hoopoes from your nightjars, you'll love Wild Rose and the deck is a perfect place to sip Chardonnay and chat with your hosts. *Minutes from Point Pelee National Park. Tom will also do personal birding tours.*

Rooms: 3: 2 kings with en-suite shower; 1 king (convertible to twins) with private bathroom (bath/shower).
Price: $100 – $110 double occupancy. Singles on request.
Meals: Full breakfast included. Supper occasionally provided if requested nicely! Birding packages include all meals.
Directions: Leave Hwy 401 at exit 63 towards Tilbury, then take Kent Rd 1 to Wheatley. Turn left at the first traffic light in Wheatley, then turn right after 500m onto Harbour Road. Wild Rose is third on the right.
Closed: Late October to March.

Map Number: 9

Aubergine Bed & Breakfast

Kathy See
67 Brunswick St, Stratford N5A 3L9
Tel: 519-275-2170 Fax: 519-275-2650
Email: aubergine@cyg.net Web: www.bbcanada.com/aubergine

A "quest for adventure" first lured Kathy to Canada and 43 years later this spirit still pervades Aubergine. Built in 1869 as a Latter Day Saints Church, an unassuming exterior gives no hint of the phantasmagoria within. Entering the vast main room is like stumbling onto the set of some bohemian play, the riot of props the vision of some idiosyncratic set-designer. Afghan rugs, an alarmingly muscle-bound 1960s Superwoman and a part of the Forest of Arden (salvaged from a production of *As You Like It*) are just a few of the whimsies. Everywhere you look something unusual catches the eye: painted wooden floors, exposed antique metal air ducts, a bedroom cupboard that doubles as a balcony – somehow it all works and comfort is never compromised. The two bedrooms reminded me of a seaside cottage with their pristine linens, wicker chairs, tongue-and-groove ceilings and over-laden bookshelves. I particularly liked the 'floating' room with its bizarre pod-like shower and windows onto the interior. Aubergine is an aesthetic feast and it is no surprise that Kathy's regulars fight over dates. *She prefers to rent the open-plan house out as a whole to people travelling together. If you only want one room, she will do a bit of matchmaking and find suitable housemates or else ensure that you are the only guests. Stratford's theatre festival from April-October is very popular.*

Rooms: 2: both queens, one has shower, one has bath and shower.
Price: $400 per night for the whole house. $200 for one room if house otherwise empty. Mid-week rates greatly reduced in May, June and October.
Meals: Full breakfast included. There is a kitchen for guests to prepare other meals.
Directions: Enter Stratford on Hwy 7/8, which turns into Ontario St. Turn left onto Waterloo St, and Aubergine is at 2nd traffic lights at intersection with Brunswick St.
Closed: Mid-Nov to mid-April. One room open in winter for regulars.

Map Number: 9

Blackwater House

Judith Horner and Hammond Bentall
RR3, Stratford N5A 6S4
Tel: 519-393-5953 Fax: 519-393-5962
Email: bwh@quadro.net

On arrival, after being greeted by, or tripping over, Jackson and Briggs (a pair of enthusiastic Jack Russells), you are likely to find a gin and tonic or a glass of wine being thrust into your hand, by either Hammond or Judith. Warm, humorous, mildly mad, and seriously good company, it's very easy to kick back and settle in here for an extended period. You have the run of the house, from the sofas in the sitting room, to the drawing room with its mouth-watering English antiques like the Carlton House writing desk. This is the oldest house in the county, built in 1854, and the planned five-year renovation was condensed into one brief year. A mix of old country-house floral fabrics, beautiful furniture and less conventional touches, like the exposed original stone wall that runs along the inside of the house, make for a happy and harmonious home. Judith's watercolours are a journal of their travels and cover the walls of the staircase and landing. Space is made for other bits of art from near and far, including a set of beautiful woodcuts and Hammond's photography – he loves chairs. Just a few minutes drive from the theatres and restaurants in Stratford, these seven acres with river, pool, gardens, orchards, extensive and gorgeous views are a must. *There are cats: Fortnum and Mason.*

Rooms: 2: 1 en-suite room in the house; 1 room with separate entrance with bed, sitting room and kitchen.
Price: $150 – $185. No single rates.
Meals: Full breakfast included.
Directions: From Stratford follow Highway 8 west to Sebringville (signed Goderich) for 7 km. Over bridge in centre of village, turn left onto Station Rd (opposite church). After 2 km road forks at Y junction. Blackwater House is on left on the bend. Fire Number 4815.
Closed: Mid-October to last weekend in May.

Jakobstettel Guest House

Ella Brubacher
16 Isabella Street, St Jacobs N0B 2N0
Tel: 519-664-2208 Fax: 519-664-1326
E-mail: info@jakobstettel.com Web: www.jakobstettel.com

Guests are very much free-range at this 1898 colonial-style mansion. Ella insists they be 'on their own time and do their own thing'. If you sleep in and miss breakfast – no problem, just help yourself. The kitchen is a free-for-all, including, rather dangerously I thought, the cookie jar. You can while away the long summer days in the five-acre garden with its pool, tennis court, croquet, volleyball, badminton and horseshoe pit. Or the more leisurely can read one of the library's numerous books in the shade of the towering pines. In winter, when the prospect of a two-setter palls, the playground moves indoors. TV is an absentee here and the wood-panelled library with its fire becomes a social hub where backgammon, chess or crokinole could all be on the evening's agenda. If you've never come across the latter before, you'll soon be a fierce competitor. The 12 rooms boast brass or wooden beds, shuttered windows and locally-made quilts and are all named after local pioneers. The undulating farmland around St Jacobs has long been the heart of Old Order Mennonite country, so don't be surprised to find yourself dodging the traditional horses and buggies on the way there. *Nature trails and farmers' markets nearby. Cross-country skiing and skating.*

Rooms: 12: 10 queens, 2 twins. All have en-suite bathrooms, most with bath/shower.
Price: $95 – $200 double occupancy. Single rates on request.
Meals: "Deluxe" Continental breakfast included. Other meals can be provided (for groups only) by prior arrangement; good restaurants within walking distance.
Directions: From Hwy 401, take Hwy 8 west towards Kitchener, then Hwy 86 north through Waterloo following 'St Jacobs Country' signs. Take either exit to St Jacobs (Road 15 or 17) and turn west in the village at Albert St. Guest house is two blocks ahead.

Map Number: 9

Ontario

Willow Manor

Donna Cooper and Jean Hill

408 Willow Rd, Guelph
N1H 6S5
Tel: 519-763-3574
Fax: 519-763-4531
Web:
www.willowmanorbb.com

Don't be surprised if it takes you a few goes to find Willow Manor. This really is a hidden gem and even most locals remain unaware of its whereabouts. Tucked away among tall trees in lush gardens, it's no surprise that many drive past for years without ever noticing it. Once located, the gardens are the first thing to catch the eye. Donna tells me the 1860 ivy-clad manor was once a large farm; no horses roaming the gardens today though, just happy guests. Herb gardens, a pool and a large hammock hanging invitingly under the maple, beech and apple trees make this a prime relaxation spot. Since Donna is also a nutritionist you'll probably find a few of the herbs have strayed onto your breakfast plate, along with delicious home-made granola, piles of fruit and perhaps a local Mennonite sausage (that's made by, not made of…). The emphasis is on health here, although you'll be glad to hear the cookie jar is never empty. The interior has the feel of a grand English country house with fresh, pale colours, wooden floors and high ceilings. The luxurious rooms vary from the ladies' favourite 'Springtime' to the bold 'Striped Room'. With its smart blue-striped walls and huge window on to the garden this was my favourite. Whether away on business or pleasure, this is a spot well worth finding.

Rooms: 4: 1 queen with jacuzzi and shower; 1 double with jacuzzi and shower; 2 kings with jacuzzis and shower.
Price: $90 – $110 double occupancy.
Meals: Full breakfast included.
Directions: 13 km north on Highway 6 from 401. Take Willow Rd exit west. B&B on corner immediately on left (south).

WeatherPine Inn B&B

Rob and Luci Vaandering

493 Regent St, PO Box 195, Niagara-on-the-Lake L0S 1J0
Tel: 905-468-5154
Email: info@weatherpine.com Web: www.weatherpine.com

Rob and Luci retired from their business in town, "and then got bored of retiring", so started the new venture of WeatherPine four years ago. This Cape Cod board-and-baton house, with its double tiers of wraparound verandahs, is a traffic-stopping feast for the eyes. In summer, hanging baskets creak, groan and grumble under the weight of blossoming wave petunias, geraniums and a multitude of other plants, different every year. The display is equally splendid in winter when the house is hung with garlands, swags of cedar and Christmas lights. There's an informal, country house feel, breakfasts spilling into brunches, and all overseen by boxer Harley and his pal, the recently-rescued Happy. Niagara-on-the-Lake is a tranquil and cultured lakeside town awash with theatres, wineries, shops and fine food. But stay with the Vaanderings, a really nice couple whose guests are made to feel properly welcome, to add good company and hearty breakfasts to the mix. Most guests will make those important decisions about where to eat tonight and what to do tomorrow over an evening's glass of wine with Rob and Luci on one of the verandahs. Not just a room and a meal. *Niagara-on-the-Lake is a busy place, book well in advance.*

Rooms: 5 queens, 2 with en-suite bathroom, 1 with en-suite shower and 1 with en-suite shower sauna.
Price: $135 – $225.
Meals: Full breakfast included.
Directions: Heading east on Queen St, in the centre of Niagara-on-the-Lake, take right onto Regent St. WeatherPine is opposite the Pillar and Post Inn.

Inn on the Twenty

Helen Young

3845 Main Street, Jordan L0R 1S0
Tel: 905-562-5336; toll-free 1-800-701-8074 Fax: 905-562-3232
Email: vintners@niagara.net Web: www.innonthetwenty.com

Winery-owners, restaurateurs and now inn-keepers, Helen Young and husband Leonard Pennachetti are double-handedly bringing life back to the old winery village of Jordan. Helen looks after the inn on one side of the main street, Leonard masterminds the Cave Spring Cellars operation on the other, with the restaurant (great views from upstairs) and shops dotted around. 'Twenty' references abound because the area, named by Loyalists fleeing the US after the War of Independence, is 20 miles from Niagara, and Jordan is an ideal spot if you want to base yourself away from the Niagara maelstrom. The inn is in an old warehouse, so it does not have the most poetic of exteriors, but the lack of architectural strictures meant that Helen was able to do pretty much what she wanted with the interiors. As a result, the rooms are very special; combinations of vibrant sofas and bedspreads, high pale walls and bathrooms that vary from the merely extravagant to the palatial. Five have private gardens with trees and wooden benches – nothing plastic here. And another five are in the 1840-built Vintage House right next door. *Talks, seminars and wine tours often available at weekends.*

Rooms: 31: 24 in the main inn, 2 in the Winemaker's Cottage, 5 in the Vintage House. Variety of suites and rooms, most king-size beds, all with en-suite bathrooms.
Price: $139 – $350 double occupancy. Singles $129 – $340.
Meals: Breakfast: 'enhanced' Continental included, extra for eggs/bacon etc. Lunch and dinner available à la carte in the restaurant.
Directions: Take Exit 57 off the QEW and follow Victoria Ave south to the traffic light at Regional Road 81. Turn left onto RR 81 and continue through Jordan Valley to Jordan proper. After leaving the valley turn left onto Main St and the inn is down on the right.
Closed: Christmas.

Map Number: 9

Denwycke House

Patricia and John Hunter
203 Main St East, Grimsby L3M 1P5
Tel: 905-945-2149 Fax: 905-945-6272
Email: johnpathunter@cs.com Web: www.denwycke.com

Just the kind of place we like – a house with history, rooms with élan, and owners with a past (in the most positive sense!). After 30 years in Ottawa, the Hunters moved to Grimsby in 1997 having fallen head over heels for Denwycke House, a beautiful Georgian-style building built in 1842. John's work for the Federal Government has taken him and Pat all over the world and consequently Denwycke's interior hosts a smorgasbord of international goodies – Russian paintings, Scottish crockery, Palestinian glassware, Jordanian rugs – together with wood panelling, beams and some stunning 19th-century furniture. There are just two suites upstairs, named after previous owners of the house. Both have wooden floors, rugs, antique furniture, sitting rooms and pretty bathrooms (full of "Victorian what-nots" in Pat's words), and the beds benefit from her remarkable quilting skills. The larger Barbour suite also has a small balcony and fireplace. There is much to do near here, with 40 wineries in the area and Niagara 30 minutes away, but don't rush in and out of Denwycke – John and Pat are far too interesting and, well, far too nice for that! They know everything about the house and the area, and love to convert new arrivals to their passion. Resistance is pointless.

Rooms: 2 suites: both have king-size beds, sitting rooms and en-suite bath/shower.
Price: $125 – $175 double occupancy. Singles $105 – $135.
Meals: Full breakfast included.
Directions: Turn off the QEW at the sign to Bartlett St (exit 68) and follow the road south. Turn right at the traffic lights (onto Main St East). The house is after 1/4 mile on the right and has a low stone wall in front. Entrance is at the end of the wall.

At Terrace House Bed and Breakfast

Suzanne Charbonneau

52 Austin Terrace, Toronto
M5R 1Y6
Tel: 416-535-1493
Fax: 416-535-9616
Email:
terracehousebandb@sympatico
Web: www.terracehouse.com

Originally from Quebec, Suzanne has settled in Toronto, via the circuitous route of Tunisia, Belgium and Washington DC. Her guests, who tend to return again and again, are glad she has. Her passion for travelling has exotically flavoured both her house and her cooking. North African rugs, tapestries and artefacts are scattered liberally around the house, while food is filled with unlikely combinations of herbs and spices. One is luxuriously woken from a bright, homely room by the wafting aromas of gently-baking bread and quiche and fresh coffee. Downstairs, piles of newspapers and a fair feast await. On the weekend, we lazed around the breakfast table for hours. Suzanne and Pierre tell me that they like to give people something that they don't necessarily get at home, and that is certainly true. Extraordinary fruit and yoghurts, fresh market treats and special breads and cereals are just part of the fabulous breakfast whose pièce de résistance is the quiche that raised you from slumber earlier. Convivial company around a large breakfast table, and conversation in both French and English keep you on your toes. Although now fully fortified for the day ahead, I'd be amazed if anyone ever gets any of the sightseeing (which is right on your doorstep) done when staying here – it's just too comfortable!

Rooms: 3: 1 double with en-suite shower; 1 double with private bath/shower; 1 king (converts to twins) shares the private bathroom if guests travelling together.
Price: $145 – $195 for single or double occupancy.
Meals: Very full breakfast included.
Directions: Austin Terrace is near Casa Loma. Directions available when booking.

Map Number: 9

The Coach House

Margot Dawson

117 Walmer Road, Toronto
M5R 2X8
Tel: 416-899-0306
Fax: 416-916-0997
Email:
margot.dawson@thecoach
house.ca
Web: www.thecoachhouse.ca

Step off Walmer Road in the central Annex area of downtown Toronto, and find yourself in a leafy, calm haven. Built in 1902, The Coach House has had a checkered career, from carriage house to children's clubhouse to a shelter for a family of racoons. But now it has been transformed, along with the third-floor apartment, by amateur painter and sculptor Margot and her husband Ian. By hand. They started the work ten years ago on behalf of their children and friends, but now you get to enjoy it too. Margot has created two very distinct styles: the ivy-clad French country cottage, surrounded by pots of geraniums in a hosta-filled garden; and the calm, spacious retreat of a tranquil Japanese apartment, with ebony wood furniture, cream walls and vivid splashes of colourful art. It's a very tricky choice. Whichever you decide, after a day spent touring the city from your doorstep, this is a place to settle back and relax. With a crammed goodie bag waiting for you, I can see why people are tempted to stay for months… and not a racoon in sight, by the way. *Margot does not do meals, but there are fridges and microwaves provided, plus full oven in the apartment and counter cook top in The Coach House. Toronto's finest eateries are nearby.*

Rooms: 2 suites: each has queen bed, sitting room, kitchen, bath/shower. Coach House has extra sofa-bed (queen); apartment has extra chair-bed (single).
Price: $175 double for stays of 1-2 nights. $150 double for stays of 3-6 nights. Weekly and monthly rates available.
Meals: No meals, but juice, wine, scones, coffee and tea provided on arrival.
Directions: Available when you book.

Toronto Downtown Bed and Breakfast

Roger Kershaw and Jim Lingerfelt
57 Chicora Avenue, Toronto M5R 1T7
Tel: 416-921-3533; toll free 1-877-950-6200
Email: info@tdbab.com Web: www.tdbab.com

Here I was greeted with the tricky choice of champagne or wine. Sinking into a sofa, surrounded by paintings by Torontonian artists and laden bookcases, I pondered whether there wasn't something meet and right about the way that Jim with his dry sense of humour was enjoying a tipple of the red, and Roger, who bubbles with energy, was on the champagne. Both are hugely entertaining, welcoming and very obviously love what they do: meeting people, organising food tours, pub crawls, theatres and restaurants, trips to Niagara, airport pick-ups, anything and everything! They look after you, but also entertain royally with liberal helpings of hysterical stories and fabulous one-liners. The huge "Celebrity Suite" with four-poster has its own roof terrace with views of the city's skyline and the CN Tower, but all rooms are sumptuously luxurious. Big travellers themselves, they've "stolen the best bits". Provisions range from cell phones to sewing kits to toothbrushes; you hardly need to pack. Roger doesn't cook as he "likes the guests to leave alive". This task is left to Jim and it's impossible to leave a mouthful. A baked apple wrapped in filo pastry with walnut butterscotch disappeared with embarrassing speed – only to be replaced with the "main course", a brie and Portobello mushroom omelette. Equally delectable, it too was despatched without delay. A difficult place to leave.

Rooms: 3: all queens, 1 with private bath/shower; 2 with en-suite bath/shower.
Price: $159 – $249 US DOLLARS.
Meals: Full breakfast included.
Directions: Ask when booking.

Saucy Willow Inn

Penny Johansen
6 Nipissing St, Coboconk K0M 1K0
Tel: 705-454-1218 Fax: 705-454-8302
Email: saucywlo@hotmail.com Web: http://saucywillow.com

This fresh, airy house was renovated – well, virtually completely rebuilt – by Penny and a motley crew of builders from her cottage base next door. The result, solely for guests, is fabulous. The ten-month project saw the charming original features of the building like the balconies, fireplaces and wooden floors retained and restored, but all possible modern wants, needs and luxuries were also catered for. Upstairs, large bedrooms with white-painted floorboards and luxurious linen are deeply restful. Difficult decisions have to be made: a private balcony or a double whirlpool tub? Downstairs a sitting room, filled with opulent, comfortable sofas and chairs clustered around a log fireplace, opens into a large hall and out onto a sunny verandah. There is a massive open-plan kitchen and breakfast room ruled by Penny. She loves to cook (and bizarrely admits to liking ironing too…), quite a change from the real-estate broker of five years ago. The sleepy town's population grows from 600 to 5,000 in summer, and Penny, who has boundless energy, also runs a restaurant at the inn. Gardens slope down to the River Gull where the willow is looking a little dishevelled due to a couple of harsh storms and over-exuberant "Edward Scissorhands" style pruning, but it's saucy enough to battle on. *Kayaks, canoes and boat moorings available. Also, self-catered 2- or 3-bedroom cottages with meals optional at the inn.*

Rooms: 7: 1 suite (1 queen with sofa bed), 5 queens, 1 twin; 3 en-suite whirlpool-jacuzzi/shower, 2 en/s showers, 1 private bath/sh, 1 private shower.
Price: $110 – $225 single or double occupancy.
Meals: Full breakfast included. Lunch and dinner à la carte in the restaurant, on request weekdays. Café open Jul & Aug for weekend dining on verandah.
Directions: Travelling north through Coboconk on Hwy 35, turn left onto Albert St and look out for the large sign on the left.
Closed: November to May.

Stone Hedge Farm

Bernie and Jim Davis
RR 1, Minden K0M 2K0
Tel: 705-286-1709 Fax: 705-286-4574
Email: sivad@interhop.net Web: www.bbcanada.com/2153.html

An unassuming red letterbox indicates that you have arrived at the farm, and a wooded driveway takes you up to the homestead. "Nothing fancy" is a favourite expression of Bernie's. I feel that I may have to differ, especially when applied to breakfast. Mexican frittatas with a multitude of fillings, sweet pink grapefruit, seven grain porridge and freshly baked breads are all on the menu, and while the oven is hot, delectable corn muffins are made. For later. Just in case you ever need food again. Jim and Bernie run their two simple Shaker style B&B rooms on a very relaxed basis, as they do a lot of touring on their bikes. If you time it right you may get to stay with them. Or stay in their holiday cottage next door, which you can make your own. Both homes overlook the farm. Traditional wooden barns house chickens, sheep and cows, all of whom roam freely over the 300 or so acres, and I encourage you to join them. Trails wriggle through the farm, the woodlands and down to the lake. The land here is stunning, and a real lesson in Canadian history and geology. 50-acre plots, the old pioneer settlements, are strewn over the glacial landscape, ancient, twisted, scraggly fruit trees and piles of rocks are the only standing reminders. Bears, mooses, coyotes and birds galore; woods, lakes, pasture and a hot tub under the stars. All the best of Canada.

Rooms: 1 self-catering cottage with 3 bedrooms. Also 2 rooms in the house sharing 1 bathroom.
Price: For the cottage: $1000 – $1100 per week in summer; please enquire about (very reasonable) daily and non-summer rates.
Meals: Self-catering in the cottage. Full breakfast for rooms in the house.
Directions: Stone Hedge Farm is between Minden and Haliburton. Call for directions.

Map Number: 9

Selwyn Shores Waterfront Bed and Breakfast

Martha and Dan Crawford

2073 Selwyn Shores Drive, RR 3, Lakefield K0L 2H0
Tel: 705-652-0277; toll-free 1-877-735-9967 Fax: 705-652-3389
Email: sleep@selwynshores.com Web: www.selwynshores.com

I walked into Martha and Dan's home and was greeted by a stupendous view of Chemong Lake, its far shores and the Ojibwe First Nation Reserve, all turning a mad lilac and orange with the sunset. This was the perfect Canadian evening. Clear skies, the first day of fall, leaves just beginning to turn, *and* arrowheads of honking geese migrating overhead. Text-book! I was bowled over by it. They say that they never tire of this view from the house, and that it is different every day. The ground floor sitting room (one of three!) from which you can decide whether this is true or not is vast with vaulted ceilings, sunken sofas and large windows — a far cry from the 9-bathroomed, 3-bedroomed, bird-occupied house they bought. In warmer weather a favourite spot to sit and be contemplative is on the end of the dock surrounded by water. Or in the comfortable, unfussy bedrooms. The lakefront location is superb and the fishing great (rods can be borrowed). If Dan is around, and not busy winning fishing tournaments, he will show you the best spots. There is also a canoe, kayak and paddleboat. Lots of opportunity to burn off a deliciously scrumptious breakfast. Martha has had a catering company for years… entertaining by profession, entertaining by nature. You are in extremely good hands!

Rooms: 5: 3 queens, 1 king and 1 twin; 2 have en-suite bath/shower, 3 share 2 more bath/shower.
Price: $85 – $105 double occupancy. Singles less $5.
Meals: Full breakfast included.
Directions: From Selwyn, go westbound on Hwy 20, then turn right on 12th Line. Turn left onto Selwyn Shores Drive and look for the totem pole.

Map Number: 9

Lilac Lane B&B

Mariann and Matthew Marlow
1738 Chemong Rd, Peterborough K9J 6X2
Tel: 705-876-8000 Fax: 705-748-9973
Email: mmarlow@sympatico.ca Web: www.bbcanada.com/lilaclane

I encountered a few of my favourite Canadian things at Lilac Lane. Firstly, Mariann herself, gorgeous, generous and filled with smiles; and secondly her son Matthew's donuts – Jamie Oliver, stand aside. They live just outside bustling Peterborough in an 1860s house, built of stone excavated during the building of the local railway. The original porch of the house has been converted to the breakfast room. With thick stone walls, wood floors and windows all around, some of which look inside to the kitchen – others across the paddock and valley beyond – it's a lovely sunny place to start the day. Shafts of morning sun stream into the room, somehow already familiar, with its pine chests, dried flowers, plants and a charming old baker's cabinet. Early risers may get to see Mariann collecting the morning's eggs among the hens and the rooster Charlie who can be rather, um, fowl. His wives quietly scratch the dirt around one of those gorgeous Canadian weatherboard barns. It's home to three cats, a couple of pony traps, bits of old aeroplane, painful-looking turnip-peelers, a threshing machine, chairs, tables, beams, windows and other ordinary and extraordinary bits of architectural salvage. Projects galore. Slowly, but surely, they will be lovingly restored and promoted to the house, like the beautifully chunky church doors in the sitting room. A personable and charming home.

Rooms: 3: 1 queen with en-suite bathroom, 1 queen with private/shared 4-piece bathroom, 1 double with private/shared 4-piece bathroom.
Price: $75 – $115 double occupancy.
Meals: Full breakfast included.
Directions: Head north out of Peterborough on Chemong Rd for about 2 miles. Keep eyes peeled for a sign on right-hand side. House is set back from the road.

Ontario

Resonance

Anna and Bob Keating

1125 Division Road, RR 1, Douro K0L 1S0
Tel: 705-742-6885 Fax: 705-742-6388
Email: resonance@sympatico.ca Web: www3.sympatico.ca/resonance

Thomas Rahalley was the original Irish settler whose location ticket landed him in the log-cabin 'shanty', which has now been renovated by Anna, a refreshingly uncontrived conversationalist with eclectic interests, and Bob, gentle giant, teacher of Taoist Tai Chi and resident minstrel. I'm afraid that Thomas, along with the cows and pigs, branch roof and straw insulation, is long gone. Instead you will have to make do (I'm sure you'll manage somehow) with a king-size bed draped with quilts, fluffy towelling robes, a heart-shaped whirlpool for two, a fire, games and thick carpets. You will have no need to leave your self-sufficient cabin, but the draw of the verandah at the main house is strong. Hammocks, rocking-chairs covered in cushions, and jolly company are the pulls. Resonance is a place that makes you slow down and appreciate nature. Birds, crickets and spring-peepers (they're frogs) sing a fabulous chorus while the sun goes down. Beefalo (yes, an official breed I'm told) ruminate in the surrounding meadows, and many vegetables are home-grown. Anna is a magnificent cook with an arsenal of suggestions and will make you meals or stock the fridge in the fully-equipped kitchen for you with prior notice. Abundant breakfasts can be served poolside, in the shade of an apple tree or amid birdsong on the verandah. *Plenty of activities including star-gazing, bird-watching, swimming, picnicking, biking, kayaking and antiquing.*

Rooms: 1 suite with en-suite therapeutic airjet whirlpool.
Price: $115 – $150. Inquire about single and long-term rates.
Meals: Full breakfast. Can do anything if arranged in advance.
Directions: From Peterborough take Hwy 134 north for 3 km. Turn right onto Division Rd. About 2 km to number 1125, second farm on the right.

Butternut Inn

Bob and Bonnie Harrison

36 North St, Port Hope L1A 1T8
Tel: 905-885-4318; toll-free 1-800-218-6670 Fax: 905-885-5464
Email: info@butternutinn.com Web: www.butternutinn.com

This happy old house, lovingly nurtured by Bonnie and Bob over the past eight years, is named after the large tree which spreads imperiously above the garden. In summer months, you'll spend most of your time out here, admiring the Harrisons' horticultural skills, watching the birds, growling at the squirrels and listening to the church bells (virtuoso performance at 12 noon!). Bob uses the fallen butternuts for golfing practice and would be delighted if you would join him, although if you felt like hoeing instead, he wouldn't object. Inside, the plant-filled solarium and sitting-room provide other charming places to ponder the world and admire Bonnie's collection of quirky dolls. While in the winter, the wood-stove in the solarium will soon persuade you to sit and read. The 1847 house was once home to the Great Farini, a legendary circus performer and impresario who walked across Niagara Falls several times, and my favourite room is named in his honour. This dashing purple affair has original pine floorboards, several African sculptures and a private whirlpool bath down the hall. The other three rooms, all stately and comfortable with wide pine floors and antique furniture, showcase a variety of themes inspired by Bob and Bonnie's travels. A friendly, relaxing place indeed. *Very popular gourmet weekends available, run by an expert chef and including accommodation, dining and lessons.*

Rooms: 4 queens: 1 with en-suite bath/shower, 2 with en-suite shower, 1 with private whirlpool/shower.
Price: $110 – $150 double occupancy. Singles usually $10 less.
Meals: Full breakfast included. Suppers available as part of gourmet weekends, or prepared by Bonnie for parties of 8 (by prior arrangement).
Directions: From Toronto: leave Hwy 401 at exit 461 and take Hwy 2 to Pine Street. Turn left. From Kingston, use exit 464. Turn right at the T-junction with Walton Street, then turn right into Pine Street. North Street is after two blocks on your right.

Hill and Dale Manor

Ontario

Jeanne and David Henderson
47 Pine St South, Port Hope L1A 3E6
Tel: 905-885-5992; toll-free 1-877-238-9132 Fax: 905-885-6467
Email: inquire@hillanddalemanor.com Web: www.hillanddalemanor.com

The entrance to Hill and Dale Manor is certainly impressive. Sweep through stone gates and up the drive to a stately, pale-coloured brick residence that sits regally on a hilltop overlooking Port Hope. Inside, it's a luxurious place too. From the extensive verandah, a large hall takes you into the heart of the house. This welcoming room leads into a sumptuous sitting room, light, opulent and very comfortable, and to the plum-panelled dining room. Here guests savour their morning feast under the watchful eyes of Henry Covert, former occupant and president of the Midland Railway, which used to stop and drop visitors at the original northern gates. His portrait – found at a local auction by Jeanne – hangs on the wall. 150 years on, Henry can't seem to take his eyes off the breakfast. David and Jeanne run a fabulous place, at a frenetic pace. In-between hunting down antiques and treasures at auction, packing children off to university and sponsoring local craft competitions (the resulting exquisite and extraordinary quilts adorn the walls of the house), an inexhaustible and invariably good-humoured Jeanne still finds time to cater to all the possible wants and needs of her many guests. She tells me with a smile that each year she gets a little slower, but I'm not sure I believe her!

Rooms: 6: 1 king and 5 queens; all with en-suite bath/shower.
Price: $110 – $159 double occupancy. Singles from $96.
Meals: Full breakfast included.
Directions: From Toronto: leave Hwy 401 at exit 461 and take Hwy 2 to Pine Street South. Turn right. Go down the hill and house is on the left. (From Kingston, use exit 464 off the 401. Turn right at the T-junction with Walton Street, then turn left into Pine Street South.)

Map Number: 9

54

Butler Creek Country Inn

Kenneth Bôsher and Burke Friedrichkeit

RR 7, Hwy 30-202, Brighton K0K 1H0
Tel: 613-475-1248; toll-free 1-877-477-5827 Fax: 613-475-5267
Email: butlerbb@reach.net Web: www.butlercreekcountryinn.com

This is a truly elegant 1905 farmhouse, a delight both inside and out. The only remaining sign that it was once a farm is the lovely old barn, and this no longer houses beasts of the flesh-and-blood variety. Now, a different kind of horse-power lurks inside: a 1955 Cadillac Fleetwood, completely original, cavernous, and definitely my favourite; and an equally delicious, red-and-white Buick, the indisputable choice of Ken and Burke, your friendly hosts. Ken is the driver and, if you are lucky, nice or fun, you may get taken for a spin. You can spend the day exploring the Apple Route and the evolving wineries in the area, or else just enjoy the charms of Butler Creek, reading, paddling and strolling in the garden that drops dramatically away behind the house. A big and very beautiful bundle of black wool may accompany you on your rambles. Blinky, a Bouvier des Flandres, is a fine guide who will show you along the mown trails that wind around the property. The creek is full of trout and in spring salmon come here to spawn. You may even get to eat one. Burke is a mean chef, whose breakfast specialities include eggs Benedict and apple pancakes. *Ken and Burke do gourmet evenings during the winter specializing in German cuisine – book in advance.*

Rooms: 6: 1 king, 5 queens; 2 have en-suite bath/shower, 1 has en-suite loo, 4 share 2 bathrooms (with bath/shower).
Price: $75 – $115 double occupancy. Singles $65 – $115.
Meals: Full breakfast included. Gourmet dinners available on request (Nov to April; from $99 per person including accommodation; 4 people minimum).
Directions: Leave Hwy 401 at exit 509 and drive south on Hwy 30 for about 3 km. Butler Creek is on the right-hand side.

Map Number: 9

The Waring House Inn and Cookery School

Christopher and Norah Rogers

Loyalist Parkway, Highway 33, PO Box 20024, Picton K0K 3V0
Tel: 613-476-7492; toll-free 1-800-621-4956 Fax: 613-476-6648
Email: waringhouse@sympatico.ca Web: www.waringhouse.com

Prince Edward County is often likened to England with its undulating hills and winding lanes. In fact you can even get Cox's orange pippins here. The beaches, however, are definitely more Caribbean with clear waters and white sand stretching for miles. A great central place from which to explore the county, with all its museums, artisans, galleries and vineyards, is the Waring House Inn, run by Norah and Christopher Rogers. The original 19th-century farmstead houses the pub, restaurant and my four favourite rooms. All the bedrooms are painted and papered in warm colours and are decorated with antiques suitable to the period of the house. The gothic arched landing window gives great views across the recently-planted vineyard (this year produced the first bottle) and the countryside beyond. Other bedrooms and suites are in a separate building on the other side of the small creek that meanders through the property. Most of these have private balconies. Acclaimed cooking classes are run in the hands-on cookery school, concentrating on cuisine from around the world and using local produce, like the Lake Ontario perch and, of course, the aforementioned pippins. *Prince Edward County is one of the best bird-watching areas anywhere and is on the Monarch butterfly migration route. You can see llamas and ostriches too.*

Rooms: 17: 4 rooms in main house; 12 in adjacent building; 1 stone cottage with vineyard view; some with air-jet tubs, outdoor hot tubs & fireplaces.
Price: $110 – $200 double occupancy. Singles $100 – $200. Cookery School packages available.
Meals: Fine dining in the restaurant, or casual dining in the pub. Breakfast is not included in the room price, except mid-week in winter. Sunday buffet brunch.
Directions: On Highway 33 between Picton and Wellington just outside Bloomfield. You will see a large sign to the west of Picton.
Closed: First week of Jan.

The Secret Garden

Maryanne and John Baker

73 Sydenham St South, Kingston K7L 3H3
Tel: 613-531-9884 Fax: 613-531-9502
Email: baker@the-secret-garden.com Web: www.the-secret-garden.com

The Secret Garden, built as a family home in 1888 by a leather and fur merchant, is a couple of blocks from central Kingston. The quiet leafy road is a leisurely evening's stroll from the high street with its restaurants, theatres and galleries. John and Maryanne run the place together and very obviously love looking after their guests. And they take great pride in their home. It's high Victorian with swing seats on the porch, floral fabrics mixed with regency stripes, dark-wood antiques, oil paintings and stained-glass windows. Some of these are original features of the house, like the panel above the door, and others are designed by Maryanne and made, as a hobby, by her talented son. Maryanne makes the breakfast, has a great sense of fun, and a passion for hunting out bargains from unlikely places – a woman after my own heart. She "rescues things" and recycles them. They are reincarnated in the house a few days later, with some new useful function, looking like they have been there for years. Tea is served every day in the parlour – grab a book from the library and tuck into the home-made cookies. *Central air-conditioning in summer. Side garden for relaxing.*

Rooms: 7: 2 queens with en-suite shower; 1 queen private bath across hall; 3 queens and 1 king with private bath/shower. 4 with fireplace.
Price: $115 – $165 double occupancy. $95 – $145 singles. Cancellation policy: 72 hours notice is required.
Meals: Full breakfast included. And afternoon tea and treats.
Directions: Exit 615 on Hwy 401 south to Johnson St for 2 km. Take a right on Sydenham St to number 73 opposite church on corner.
Closed: Christmas.

Rosemount Inn

Holly Doughty and John Edwards

46 Sydenham St South, Kingston K7L 3H1
Tel: 613-531-8844; toll-free 1-888-871-8844 Fax: 613-544-4895
Email: rosemt@kingston.net Web: www.rosemountinn.com

With an eye for a good property after careers working in real estate, Holly and John snapped up this 1850s Tuscan-villa-style house in 1987. They then kicked back from the hustle and bustle of office life and took on the even hustlier bustle of running a busy bed and breakfast. Imposingly situated on the corner of the street and gorgeously Italianate, with sturdy cast-iron railings, stained-glass arched leaded windows and hand-cut limestone, this is a house that stands out. The hardwood-floored rooms are decorated with floral prints, lace and luxurious linens; nooks and crannies on landings are filled with antiques. Four posters or bonnet beds, private balconies or whirlpool baths, such are the tricky choices that face you. Perhaps you can decide while sitting in the parlour drinking iced tea and eating delicious home-cooked goodies. For breakfast, crab and Swiss cheese frittatas or the intriguing house speciality of Welsh toast with berry sauce will place you in good stead to discover the 1000 Islands and Kingston's cultural delights. Very enjoyable – a relaxed home and hosts. *Wine, dine and spa packages available. An on-site spa for aromatherapy relaxation treatments is available by advance appointment.*

Rooms: 9: all queens with private bathrooms.
Price: $139 – $350 double occupancy. Single rates on request.
Meals: Full breakfast and afternoon tea and cookies included.
Directions: From Hwy 401 south on exit 619 (Montreal St) to bottom – Brock St. Right on Brock, move into left lane, take first left off Brock into Sydenham St South. Proceed two blocks.
Closed: Mid-December - early January.

A Stone's Throw

Barbara Ball

21 Earl Street, Kingston K7L 2G4
Tel: 613-544-6089
Fax: 613-544-8297
Email: info@astonesthrow.ca
Web:
www.webwoods.com/astones
throw

This lovely little limestone house is a "stone's throw" from Lake Ontario, walking trails, theatres, galleries and downtown Kingston. Built in the late 1700s it's one of the oldest buildings in town, and is a favourite place of mine. You never know who will be your breakfast companions – they could well be a kung-fu expert or a Russian mathematician – but whoever they are, they're bound to be great. Interesting people seem to gravitate here, and it's not difficult to see why. It's not just the "Art and Gourmet breakfasts", which look and taste delicious and often have people running upstairs to fetch their cameras. "I enjoy cooking," says Barbara, "and I guess it shows." Neither is it down to the house, crammed with eye-catching pieces, ancient Chinese fans framed and hung on the wall, and delectable droplet crystal lights collected by Barbara on her travels. And neither can the garden take all the credit, despite having a patio overlooking the harbour, the perfect place for summer breakfasts, afternoon tea, pre-theatre drinks, or a chat with the majestic man of the house, a golden retriever called Basil. No – the essence of A Stone's Throw is Barbara herself and we're big fans. She is sparkling and it's a pleasure to spend time in her company. *Central air-conditioning for hot summers; near Fort Henry and convenient for cruises around the harbour and Thousand Islands. Barbara has two cats by the way called Bentley and Oscar.*

Rooms: 3: 1 queen with en-suite bath/shower; 2 doubles sharing 1 bath/shower.
Price: $75 – $140 double occupancy. Singles less $10.
Meals: Full breakfast included. Will pack a lunch on request.
Directions: Take Hwy 401 to Hwy 15, south to a 'T' junction (Hwy 2). Turn right onto Hwy 2, which becomes Ontario St. Stay on Ontario St past City Hall until Earl St.

Quebec

Auberge du Vieux-Port

Dina Antonopoulos
97 rue de la Commune Est,
Old Montreal H2Y 1J1
Tel: 514-876-0081;
toll-free 1-888-660-7678
Fax: 514-876-8923
Email:
info@aubergeduvieuxport.com
Web:
www.aubergeduvieuxport.com

With its prime spot on the waterfront on one of Old Montreal's famed cobbled streets, the Auberge is ideal if you want to be right there in the hub of the old city, but indulge yourself at the same time. The scene can't have changed a bit in over a hundred years (the building dates from the 1880s). It doesn't take much to imagine the clatter of hooves and rumble of carriages in times gone by. Inside, the Antonopoulos family have created an atmosphere fitting for such surroundings. Natural materials feature heavily and the rooms are an innovative medley of rough stone walls, wooden floors, original beams and luxurious super-beds. Tall windows look out across the twinkling harbour and the various remaining exhibits from Expo '67 – namely the biosphere. My room had the added rustic feature of a barn-style wooden post, a fitting companion to the exposed walls. Downstairs, a spiral staircase descends into their award-winning restaurant, *Les Remparts*. It's one of those cosy, convivial restaurants filled with chatter and the chink of wine-glasses. My supper was seriously tasty and I heard other guests exclaiming delightedly as they ate. Furthermore, you have to love the kind of place that deals with your car, delivers the papers to your room every morning and serves you evening cocktails. *There is a rooftop terrace too.*

Rooms: 38: 27 rooms (mix of queens, kings and doubles). All en suite, mostly jacuzzis, some with showers; 11 lofts: kings with en/s bath/shower.
Price: $165 – $290 ($25 per extra person). No single rates. Children under 12 are free. Lofts $225 – $350. Ask for long-stay rates.
Meals: Full breakfast included. Award-winning restaurant on premises (fine French cuisine). Wine and cheese every evening. Rooftop terrace.
Directions: Ask when booking.

Map Number: 8 & 10

Petite Auberge les Bons Matins

Harold Côté

1393 ave Argyle, Montreal H3G 1V5
Tel: 514-931-9167; toll-free 1-800-588-5280 Fax: 514-931-1621
Email: matins@cam.org Web: www.bonsmatins.com

Upon discovering this quiet old street in downtown Montreal Harold rang every buzzer to see if anyone was selling. Where there's a will there's a way; now the Côté empire is gradually marching down Argyle Avenue leaving luxurious rooms, suites and self-catering apartments in its wake. Harold is a perfectionist who loves shopping, the perfect combination for an *aubergiste*. He may tell you that the rooms are 'stuffed with all kinds of old junk', but every detail has been carefully considered. No single style pervades – if he likes something, he buys it. Moroccan lamps and mosaic tables are mixed with Persian rugs, chunky wooden furniture, exposed brickwork and ornate marble fireplaces. Huge, vibrant canvases by Quebec-born Benoit A. Côté fill the walls and massive panelled archways divide up the suites. Old wooden doorposts framed the bed in my ultra-stylish suite and the bathroom floor was a wacky mosaicked affair. The hub of the *auberge* is the breakfast room, a warm sunny spot where guests sit around Moroccan tables reading the paper, sipping freshly-squeezed orange juice and deciding just what to eat from the cornucopia of healthy delicacies. In the evenings guests can roam freely here and help themselves from the honesty bar. A big thumbs-up all round. *Five minutes walk from Rue St Catherine and Rue Crescent.*

Rooms: 27: all king or queen beds: 9 suites (jacuzzi, fireplace, shower, 5 with kitchen); 12 rooms; and 6 apartment suites (fire, jac'zi, terrace, kitchen).
Price: $99 – $299. $20 per additional person. No single rates.
Meals: Full or Continental breakfast included.
Directions: From Toronto on 401, Hwy 20, 720 East (all heading for Montreal Centre-Ville). Take Guy St exit. First lights go right onto René Levesque Blvd. Drive thru next 2 lights to Guy. Right onto Guy. 1st street on left is Argyle Ave. Beside Day's Inn Hotel.

Hôtel Place D'Armes

Dimitri Antonopoulos

701 Côte de la Place D'Armes, Montreal H2Y 2X6
Tel: 514-842-1887; toll-free 1-888-450-1887 Fax: 514-842-6469
Email: info@hotelplacedarmes.com Web: www.hotelplacedarmes.com

Get out your Gucci, kick back with a vodka Martini and inject a bit of glamour into your holiday. Modern, stylish and very cosmopolitan, the Hôtel Place D'Armes puts the slick into the city and the hip into the hotel. Dominating one side of the Place D'Armes in Old Montreal, the building is reminiscent of a European palace with its sculptured, quasi-classical exterior and spectacular lobby. Ornately moulded pillars and vast arched windows soar upwards, dwarfing the swanky bar, its Prada-clad patrons and fold-yourself-in sofas. The cocktail of slick modern design and Victorian splendour really works. Urban chic prevails in the rooms, yet the atmosphere is still warm and inviting. Corner rooms have a penthouse feel with their three windows and panoramic city views. In others you'll find slinky black hardwood floors or exposed brick walls; the latter an interesting rustic twist in a quintessentially urban landscape. Yet with their luxurious combination of gleaming chequered floors, jacuzzis and extreme spaciousness it was the bathrooms I particularly fell for. Powdering your nose will never be such fun! Everything is provided here – rooftop gym, evening cocktails and even a downtown shuttle service every morning. All you have to do is order that next Martini. *The hotel has its own restaurant, Nava.*

Rooms: 48: 10 queen, 29 king, 4 suites and 5 with 2 doubles; all en-suite bathrooms, mix of jacuzzis, baths and showers.
Price: $175 – $600. No single rates. $25 per extra person.
Meals: Continental breakfast included. Restaurant on the premises. Wine and cheese complimentary in the afternoon. Room service.
Directions: Ask when booking.

La Sauvagine

Marianne Hubert
3813 Chemin Saint Charles, Lachenaie J6V 1A3
Tel: 450-492-0814 Fax: 450-492-6897
Email: sauvagin@ca.inter.net Web: www.gitescanada.com/4621.html

I felt more than a little nervous as I arrived here; French was never my forte and English certainly isn't Marianne's. But you don't need language to understand the charms of La Sauvagine and its delightful owner. It's one of those cosy, characterful places you immediately feel comfortable in, with lots of old wooden furniture and a real lived-in look. It's also positively prehistoric in Canadian terms, having been built in 1743 and occupied by eight generations of the same family until Marianne, an author and poet, bought it in 1991. Originally from Switzerland, it was always her dream to live in Quebec, and after recovering from illness 14 years ago she waved goodbye to the Alps and headed for Montreal. She couldn't have chosen a more authentically Quebecois house than this. Vast stone walls and roughly-hewn beams betray its age, and the rooms are the epitome of old Quebec with quilts, antique Quebecois beds and sloped beamed ceilings. The 'Zen' room adds an interesting Oriental twist. I loved the fact that nothing is quite straight and the wooden floors are delightfully crooked from generations of wear. Located only 30 minutes from downtown Montreal, this is an easy escape from city life and Marianne is a sunny, easy-going lady who you can't fail to like. *On the Mille-Isles River. Bicycles for hire. Very little English spoken here.*

Rooms: 2 queens sharing 2 bathrooms, 1 with bath and 1 with shower.
Price: $80. $25 per extra person.
Meals: Full breakfast included. 'Gastronomique' 6-course meals by advance booking $35 – $45 a head. Simple dinners at $25.
Directions: From Montreal take Autoroute 40 east, direction Quebec City and Trois Rivières. Take Exit 94. Stop sign turn right, follow road in circle over the autoroute. This is now Ch St Charles (or the 344 West). Follow for 3 km and La Sauvagine is on the right (big duck on the sign).

Au Gré du Vent B&B

Michèle Fournier and Jean L'Heureux

2 rue Fraser, Lévis G6V 3R5
Tel: 418-838-9020; toll-free 1-866-838-9070 Fax: 418-838-9074
Email: augreduvent@msn.com Web: www.bbcanada.com/augreduventbb

Quebec City is one of the most attractive towns in North America; Château Frontenac is its crowning glory… and guests of Michèle and Jean have the panorama served up to them from this large Victorian house on the south side of the St Lawrence River. Five minutes to the ferry then ten minutes on the boat take you oh-so-conveniently to the heart of the old quarter. Most guests leave their cars at the B&B for the duration of their stay and explore *à pied* as we *Greenwoodiens francophones* would have it. The house to which they return is a B&B for all the right reasons. Having left successful careers in the world of banking, Michèle and Jean now run it simply for the love of having guests. Everyone usually eats together at a large table in the yellow, natural-wood breakfast room or outside on the Quebec-facing terrace. Elsewhere there's lots of family furniture, a handsome wooden staircase, piano and paintings. The bedrooms have wooden floors and high ceilings and my favourite was probably downstairs, with its solid four-poster. 'The Castle' might claim the best views, but 'The Bathroom' offers a particular treat for those who want to gorge their eyes while they soap their thighs. As it were. *Good English spoken here.*

Rooms: 5: 3 doubles and 2 doubles plus a single; all en suite, 4 with showers and 1 with bath/shower.
Price: $95 – $110 double occ. Singles $85 – $95. Summer weekends minimum 2-night bookings. 10% rebate off-season.
Meals: Full breakfast included.
Directions: From Quebec City follow Hwy 20 to exit 325 north. Follow signs to Maison Alphonse Desjardins along Bvd Alphonse Desjardins and Côte du Passage to rue Bégin. Take Bégin to Guénette, turn left and drive to Fraser.

Maison des Gallant

Nicole Dumont and Jean Gallant

40 route du Fleuve Ouest, CP 52, Ste-Luce-sur-Mer G0K 1P0
Tel: 418-739-3512; toll-free 1-888-739-3512
Email: jean.gallant@cgocable.ca Web: www.gites-classifies.qc.ca/gallant.htm

Of all the former mayors of Quebec towns that I've ever met (two), Jean is the most down-to-earth. A happy jeans-and-shirt kind of guy, he spent four years directing civic affairs in Ste-Luce, and now works as a hospital administrator in Rimouski. He is Ste-Luce to the bone, born in the riverside house where he and Nicole operate a charming B&B. Nicole, a retired teacher, comes from the nearby town of Biencourt, whose literal meaning of "well short" explains (she says) her size. Theirs is a very relaxed house; all is in superb condition, the welcome is homely, and I felt truly at ease – or was that the maple-derived apéritif? The downstairs section of the B&B is open-plan and you eat and sit in a recently completed extension that has windows on three sides. The bedrooms are simply decorated with the odd family heirloom, and I was rather taken with the velvet bedspread that cosseted my bed. Outside, a narrow garden leads down to a gazebo at the edge of the beach, and summer evenings are often made even more memorable by camp-fires on the sand. *National Geographic magazine says (apparently!) that the sunsets in this region are the best in the world. Ste-Luce is famous for its long beach and pretty promenade, while keen divers can visit the nearby wreck of the Empress of Ireland.*

Rooms: 3: 2 doubles and 1 twin; 1 shared bathroom with bath/shower.
Price: $70 – $75 double occupancy. Singles $60 – $65. Extra person $25.
Meals: Full breakfast included.
Directions: 320 km east of Quebec City. Hwy 20 from Quebec City, then Route 132. Ste Luce is off the road to the left between Rimouski and Mont Joli. In Ste Luce they are 0.2 km west of the church, i.e. with the church on your right continue 200m upriver.

New Brunswick

Auberge Blue Heron B&B

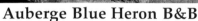

Lynne Ranger Hayes and James Hayes
24372 Route 134 du Littoral Acadien, New Mills E8G 1E6
Tel: 506-237-5560; toll-free 1-888-595-2311 Fax: 506-237-2900
Email: blueheron@bigfoot.com or auberge_blue_heron@yahoo.com
Web: www.bbcanada.com/2304.html

While some visitors will revel in the great breakfasts and dashes of humour that characterise the *auberge*, others with more scientific leanings will enjoy the ornithology, palaeontology and ecology – just a few of the 'ologies' to be sampled here. Encircled by the USA, Quebec's Gaspé Peninsula and the Acadian Coast, this northern shoulder of New Brunswick offers a cornucopia of attractions. The sea is a short stroll from the breakfast table and a profusion of wildlife is literally on your doorstep. Lush fields slope away from the Blue Heron down to the Baie des Chaleurs, home to both Heron Island, an ecological reserve (visitable on boat trips), and a mysterious Phantom Ship, a burning schooner that locals say they have seen sailing the bay before vanishing moments later. The bay is also the second oldest fossil site in the world, and the ancient Appalachian Mountains rise up behind. What's so great about the Blue Heron, however, is the accessibility of all this, and James's local knowledge makes it all the more so. Back inside, rooms are fresh and incredibly light-filled with gleaming hardwood floors and 'a little bit of whimsy'. 1920s prints, clawfoot baths, four-posters and old maps are a few of the things you could find. The pièce de résistance must be the views, although you may disagree after one of Lynne's breakfasts. *Biking, sea-kayaking, hiking, fishing, horse-riding also available.*

Rooms: 7: 5 queens with en-suite bath and shower; 1 double with private bath and shower; 1 twin double with private bath and shower.
Price: $75 – $120 double occupancy. Singles $69 – $110.
Meals: Full breakfast included.
Directions: From Bathurst, take Hwy 11 north and exit 357 to coastal Route 134 north (12 km from exit). From Campbelltown exit 375 south to Route 134 south (8.5 km from exit).
Closed: November 1st - May 1st.

Map Number: 11

Blair House Heritage Breakfast Inn

David and Judy Whittingham

38 Prince William St, St Stephen E3L 1S3
Tel: 506-466-2233; toll-free 1-888-972-5247 Fax: 506-466-1699
Email: blairhse@nbnet.nb.ca Web: www.blairhouseinn.nb.ca

David's 9 pm communion of hot chocolate, tea and biscuits is only one of the many traditions that make this a great B&B. I arrived just in time for this daily treat, and found my fellow guests exchanging travel tales over steaming mugs. David, a charming, laid-back Englishman, was busy chatting and ensuring everyone was happy. Breakfast in the sunny dining room was an equally sociable affair, although the delights emerging from the kitchen made it hard to concentrate on conversation. Such conviviality is just a bonus in a place which spoils you anyway. Named after Henrietta Blair, for whom it was built in 1860, Blair House is an ornate Italianate building, its distinctive arched windows seen on only one other house in town. Architecture aside, the style is of understated luxury. The rooms are cosy and inviting and the beds deliciously comfortable – no frills, just casual elegance. Wallowing in your claw-foot tub is personally recommended while the wide landing with its wicker chairs and bay window is a great spot to survey the USA over the St Croix River. Blair House is the last bastion of Canadian hospitality before you cross over to Maine and is everything a B&B should be. *St Stephen is a chocoholic's paradise, being the home of Ganong's Chocolatier and the Chocolate Museum.*

Rooms: 5: 3 queens, 1 double, 1 twin; all en suite, 3 with bath/shower, 2 with shower.
Price: $85 – $109 double occupancy. Singles $80 – $105.
Meals: Full breakfast included.
Directions: Enter St Stephen on Hwy 1 or 3 (south). At the 4th set of lights (Subway sandwich shop) turn left onto Prince William St. Blair House is 1/4 mile down on the left.
Closed: Christmas.

Map Number: 10 & 11

Windsor House of St Andrews

Jay Remer and Greg Cohane

132 Water Street, St Andrews E5B 1A8
Tel: 506-529-3330 Fax: 506-529-4063
Email: windsorhouse@townsearch.com
Web: www.townsearch.com/windsorhouse

Built by Loyalists in 1798, no. 132 Water Street has been reincarnated many times: private residence, hotel, boarding house and stage coach stop, it's done them all. Hence when Jay and Greg bought it in 1996, the soul of this noble old building was in a sorry state of neglect. For the next two and a half years over a hundred local craftsmen were employed in one of the largest historic renovations New Brunswick (perhaps even Canada?) has witnessed. The house was meticulously restored to its original Georgian splendour, whilst retaining some of the finer Victorian elements. Windsor House is now an inn of the highest calibre. A sojourn here combines culture and indulgence. You can admire the museum-quality art collection while sipping one of their 80 wines. Among countless other treasures the inn houses one of the largest collections of Landseer engravings in North America. And in the bedrooms perfectionism has triumphed. After you've soaked in your claw-foot tub with hand-made soaps, you'll step onto Italian marble mosaic floors. Beautiful antiques abound throughout, and every room has a fresh orchid, original wooden flooring and Persian rugs. The fact that it is one of only three 'Four Diamond' restaurants in Atlantic Canada is the icing on the cake. *St Andrews has numerous attractions including whale-watching, golf and nautical activities.*

Rooms: 6: 4 queens, 1 double, 1 twin; all en-suite bathrooms, 2 bath and shower, 4 bath/shower.
Price: $125 – $300 single or double occupancy.
Meals: Full breakfast included (brunch on Sundays). Dinner available à la carte in the restaurant.
Directions: Water Street is the main street along the waterfront. Windsor House is at 132.
Closed: January to March.

The Inn at Whale Cove Cottages

Laura Buckley

26 Whale Cove Cottage Road, North Head, Grand Manan Island E5G 2B5
Tel: 506-662-3181
Web: www.holidayjunction.com/whalecove

The inn came to be after four charismatic Bostonian ladies paid $400 for the 1816 farm in 1902. 'The Cottage Girls' became island legends through their independence and eccentricity and not since their purchase has the property changed hands for money. The equally feisty Laura inherited it from her mother, who had herself co-inherited it. As you bump down the narrow lane to the cluster of old buildings overlooking the sea, you are instantly struck by a sense of those bygone days when the 'girls' shocked islanders with their new motorcar and the ferry only went once a week. The sitting room is 'untouched since 1816' with a painted wooden floor, hand-hewn beamed ceiling and open fireplace; the bay window is made from parts of an old shipwreck; old books and antique Shaker furniture complete the effect. The bedrooms have that unmistakable seaside feel and are fresh and invigorating with bright wooden floors, crisp linens and sea breezes. Even the claw-foot tubs are a jaunty yellow. This is a place to come and re-charge the batteries and revel in nature, to enjoy the prolific birdlife and amble down beautiful trails. And also to feast on Laura's wonderful cooking which is an attraction in itself. *Great hiking trails, beaches, birding and whale-watching. Call 506-662-3724 for ferry schedules from the mainland.*

Rooms: 3 B&B rooms: 2 queens, 1 double; all en suite, 1 bath and shower, 1 bath/shower, 1 bath.
Price: $95 – $105 for B&B, single or double occupancy. Cottages are $700 – $800 per week.
Meals: Full breakfast included with B&B. Take out lunch and à la carte dining available in the restaurant. Reservations required.
Directions: Turn left off the ferry, then take Whistle Road to the right after about 400m. You'll see the sign to the inn on the right after 1 km.
Closed: November to April.

Map Number: 10 & 11

Inn on the Cove and Spa

Ross and Willa Mavis
1371 Sand Cove Road, PO
Box 3113, Stn B, Saint John
E2M 4X7
Tel: 506-672-7799;
toll-free 1-877-257-8080
Email: inncove@nbnet.nb.ca
Web: www.innonthecove.com

Innkeepers, authors and TV stars… Ross and Willa are a busy pair. Since starting the inn in 1991 they have written two cook books and shot 135 of their 'Tide's Table' cookery programmes. All were shot either at the inn or on the beach below, and have rendered them local celebrities. Ross's passion for the inn is irrepressible and he believes nurture, personal interaction and genuine warmth are vital to their guests' enjoyment. He and Willa want to provide a "retreat from reality", a haven where people are "closing the door on the rest of their world". During my stay I met one couple who were enjoying their 22nd such retreat! The emphasis is on pampering: big fluffy robes, candles, fresh flowers, deep carpets and double jacuzzis overlooking the Bay of Fundy with its legendary tides. The house itself was built in 1907 as a wedding present for Percy Manchester, Alexander Graham Bell's private gardener, and is the only waterfront property in the city complete with beach and three Suffolk sheep. Having feasted at the original 'Tide's Table', sit on your balcony and enjoy the beauty of the water sparkling in the moonlight. And make sure you leave time for the spa where you can enjoy tweaking and mud wraps galore. *Walking and Nature Trails from the inn. Next door to Irving Nature Park.*

Rooms: 4: 1 apartment with king and single, 2 queens, 1 double; all have en-suite bath/shower and the queens have jacuzzis.
Price: $85 – $195 single or double occupancy.
Meals: Full breakfast included. Spa lunch available for spa clients. Dinner available with 24 hours notice ($52.95 + $7.50 s/c) – closed Sun and Mon.
Directions: Take exit 119AB and turn right onto Bleury. At the top of Bleury turn right onto Sand Cove Road. The inn is 1/2 mile along on the left-hand side.
Closed: December 22nd - 29th.

Florentine Manor

Mary and Cyril Tingley

356 Route 915, Harvey on the Bay E4H 2M2
Tel: 506-882-2271;
toll-free 1-800-665-2271
Fax: 506-882-2936
Email: florainn@nbnet.nb.ca
Web:
www.sn2000.nb.ca/comp/
florentine-manor-b&b

Mary began saving for the beautiful white house across the street when she was ten. In 1976 her piggy bank was finally emptied onto the table and Florentine Manor was hers. By now she was married to Cyril, who she 'got across the lake', and the pair spent the next three years sanding, painting and wallpapering, a Herculean task given the size of the house. Built in the 1860s, the house has had only three owners and its most obviously striking feature is the profusion of windows, 44 in total. No bedroom has fewer than two and the refreshing result is a house infused with light. The mottled sunlight streams in through oak and birch trees and cool Bay of Fundy breezes provide natural air-conditioning. The rooms are cheery affairs with beautiful handmade quilts, gleaming wooden floors, antique beds and bucolic views. And you may find some dahlias fresh from the garden. Nineteen years on Mary still loves what she does and delights in sharing her childhood dream with her guests. Fundy National Park, Hopewell Rocks and endless other activities are within close range and Mary will happily point you in the right direction. If you want to relax and lift your spirits then head for Harvey on the Bay of Fundy. This is a place to banish those blues. *Dinner by reservation for guests only. Packed lunches can be provided.*

Rooms: 9: 2 kings, 2 queens, 1 queen and double, 1 double and single, 1 double, 1 with 3 singles, 1 twin (shower only). All the rest have en-suite bath/shower.
Price: $89 – $149 single or double occupancy.
Meals: Dinner by reservation for guests only $21.95. Market price for lobster in season. Packed lunches can be provided.
Directions: Leave Hwy 1 to take Rt 114 from Sussex to Alma. Leave Alma on Rt 915, and Florentine Manor is after 27 km on the left-hand side.
Closed: February - March.

Map Number: 11

Prince Edward Island

West Point Lighthouse

Jack Peddle
PO Box 429, O'Leary C0B 1V0
Tel: 902-859-3605; toll-free 1-800-764-6854 Fax: 902-859-1510
Email: wplight@isn.net Web: www.westpointlighthouse.com

With phantom ships, mysterious sea serpents and things that creak in the night, this is not a destination for the faint-hearted. But for gung-ho Greenwood types it is just the ticket and a stay here is certainly a unique experience. Situated at the extreme south-western tip of the island, the 68-foot lighthouse was built in 1875 and manned until 1963 when its second keeper retired. Jack, a twinkly-eyed Newfoundlander with an Irish lilt, told me with relish how the first keeper, 'Lighthouse Willie', still haunts the place. The lighthouse itself only has two guest rooms, 'The Tower' and 'Keeper's Quarters', and doubles as a museum. Photos, facts and memorabilia crowd the walls as you wind up the old wooden staircase to the Lamp Room. From here the views across the Northumberland Strait are fantastic, and the sunsets sublime. You may even get to see the flaming Phantom Ship, first sighted in 1786 (spring and fall are prime sighting times). The lighthouse is right next to Cedar Dunes Provincial Park and summer days can be spent basking on the very fine beach; the ocean is so close that you have the rare luxury of being lulled to sleep by the sound of the waves. And for weary beach-dwellers the lighthouse restaurant offers a tasty range of liquid and solid sustenance. *Great walking and beaches.*

Rooms: 9: 4 queens, 4 doubles, 1 with 2 doubles; all have en-suite bath/shower and 2 have jacuzzis.
Price: $75 – $130 for single or double occupancy. Off-season rates available. Extra person $10.
Meals: Breakfast, lunch and dinner available in the restaurant.
Directions: West Point is on Route 14 on the south-west tip of the island, right next to Cedar Dunes Provincial Park. You can't miss the lighthouse!
Closed: October to mid-May.

Silver Fox Inn

Penny and Rod Herbert

61 Granville St, Summerside C1N 2Z3
Tel: 902-436-1664; toll-free 1-800-565-4033 Fax: 902-436-1664
Email: info@silverfoxinn.net Web: www.silverfoxinn.net

After a rather unsatisfactory inn experience as a guest elsewhere, Penny decided she could do it better herself. The 'For Sale' sign outside The Silver Fox provided the perfect opportunity, and three years down the line I'm sure none of her guests have reached the same conclusion. Built in 1892 by William Critchlow Harris, PEI's foremost architect, the house was later owned by wealthy fox-breeders, hence the name. Penny and Rod have not let the standards drop and today the Silver Fox Inn is a place to wind down and lap up the luxury. My room, Platinum Fox, was divine. With its canopy and mountains of cushions the bed was my idea of heaven. Hell was having to get out of it again. Penny has thought of everything: chocolates, soaps and Evian welcome you, while the bathroom has treats such as massagers, bath pearls and hot-water bottles. Breakfast more than compensated for the trauma of having to get out of bed. Delectable little sun-dried tomato quiches and smoked salmon were on offer next to the usual breakfast fare. Thanks to Penny's sideline in antiques the inn is bursting with treasures, the porch doubling as a shop for her various finds. Guests here are thoroughly spoilt, and Penny and Rod are great fun to boot. 3 minutes walk from Downtown Summerside. *On Confederation Trail and Heritage Tour Walk.*

Rooms: 6: 3 queens, 1 with queen and single, 1 with 2 doubles, 1 double; all en-suite bath/shower.
Price: $75 – $135 for single or double occupancy. $20 for an extra person.
Meals: Full breakfast included. Dinners by reservation only. 5-course dinners approx $30 per person, 2-person minimum.
Directions: Follow Rte 1a from Confederation Bridge to Summerside. Follow Rte 11 to Downtown Summerside. Turn right onto Granville St at the lights beside the Loyalist Hotel. The Silver Fox Inn is 3 blocks up on the right.

Warn House B&B

David and Barbara Davidson

330 Central Street, Summerside C1N 3N1
Tel: 902-436-5242; toll-free 1-888-436-7512 Fax: 902-436-2442
Email: d.davidson@auracom.com Web: www.warnhouse.com

Warn House is the satisfying realisation of a 20-year dream for Barbara. While working in Ottawa, she used to wing it to Cape Cod for weekends, to 'research' B&Bs. Buying Warn House in 1999 gave the Davidsons the opportunity to put all the research into practice. Surrounded by maples, crab-apples and mountain ash, this grand colonial house is a woody hideaway – although it's hard ever to feel very urban in PEI. The wraparound verandah is a great spot to enjoy balmy summer evenings, while inside the house is cosy and welcoming. Art garnered from all corners of the world adorns the walls, evidence of David and Barbara's globetrotting. The dining room has a particularly fine collection, an impressive backdrop appropriate to David's delicious breakfasts (stratas and frittatas among other temptations). The beautiful German hand-painted grandfather clock is another world souvenir. The bedrooms are traditional and luxurious with big fluffy featherbeds and gleaming hardwood floors. I particularly liked the children's room with its jolly quilts and sweet yellow armoire, and also the bathroom towel rack in the 'Richmond room', salvaged by Barbara from a Bloomingdale's display. A great two-acre retreat to rest weary feet after a day at the beach with 'Anne of Green Gables'. *Located in the heart of Summerside, close to theatre, restaurants, College of Piping and waterfront.*

Rooms: 4: 1 king with en/s double shower; 1 queen en/s bath and shower; 1 queen en/s shower only; 1 twin/king private clawfoot bath and separate shower.
Price: $75 – $115. Ask for singles.
Meals: Full breakfast included.
Directions: From Confederation Bridge go towards Summerside on Highway 1a. Left on Water St at Summerside, follow for 3 km into downtown area. Take a right on Central St. They are 1 km on left.

Map Number: 11

Summer Garden B&B

Gail and Joe Kern

8148 Argyle Shore Rd, RR1, Bonshaw C0A 1C0
Tel: 902-675-4741 Fax: 902-675-2858
Email: gkern@isn.net Web: www.summergardeninn.com

Easy-going, humorous and warmth-exuding, Gail and Joe are one of those couples that you can't help but love. New Yorkers in a past life, they were seduced by the tranquillity of PEI one holiday and in 1978 bought 107 acres on the south shore. Joe, being a woodworker *extraordinaire*, then built the open post-and-beam house, made the furniture and even did some of the paintings that now hang on the walls. What a guy! The location is superb. Orchards, fields and their organic garden slope down towards the Northumberland Strait. In summer it's swimming, walking and cycling; in winter cross-country skiing. When I visited it was harvest time, and the kitchen was overflowing with buckets of peppers and tomatoes from the garden, awaiting dispatch to island restaurants. Evidence of real life is everywhere you look; the profusion of dried flowers in the kitchen, the stacks of books, the vibrant hand-painted furniture. Colourful quilts and wooden floors make the sea-facing bedrooms equally homely and unpretentious. Breakfast is, well, pretty special. Gail, being half-Italian, really knows how to cook. Combine this with the fact that they previously owned PEI's foremost natural health store for 25 years and you get the picture. Yum. This is somewhere to put on your straw hat, dig out your favourite book and head for the shade of an apple tree. *Private cottage scheduled for 2003.*

Rooms: 3: 1 queen and 1 double and a single share 1 bathroom; 1 queen with private bathroom. Both bathrooms are bath and shower. All sea-facing.
Price: $80 – $85 for double occupancy. No single rates. Weekly rates available.
Meals: Full breakfast included. Dinner by pre-arrangement.
Directions: From Charlottetown take Trans-Canada highway west towards Summerside. After Bonshaw take next left to Argyle Shore. At T-junction here, turn right on Route 19. Summer Garden is 3.3 km on the right-hand side, opposite Argyle Shore Provincial Park.

Map Number: 11

Shipwright Inn

Jordan and Judy Hill

51 Fitzroy St, Charlottetown CIA IR4
Tel: 902-368-1905; toll-free 1-888-306-9966 Fax: 902-628-1905
Email: innkeeper@shipwrightinn.com Web: www.shipwrightinn.com

Once ensconced at the Shipwright Inn, I soon decided the rain outside was a significant plus, not a minus. Oh well, I suppose I'll have to stay in then…! And the sight of my room also overrode any supper plans – miss out on a second of this? No way. Who needs supper anyway when there's a tantalising selection of muffins, fresh lemonade and hot chocolate to be had? I soaked in a jacuzzi, deciding which essential oil to treat myself to instead. You probably get the picture. This is a joyous, seriously pampering experience, a place to take anyone you feel needs a bit of impressing… like yourself. My room was divine and, despite the grandeur, extremely cosy. With its vast canopied bed, beautiful antiques, heavy silk curtains and wooden floors I felt like I'd stepped into the room of a Victorian nobleman. Judy's creative touch has rendered every room an aesthetic treat, but what is most appealing about the Shipwright Inn are Jordan and Judy themselves. Psychiatric social worker and occupational therapist respectively, their talent for caring is obvious and there's absolutely no stuffiness here. They'll be pouring your coffee at breakfast and serving up French toast, while their black lab Piper keeps everyone entertained with his tricks. If you don't get round to all that sightseeing, you have been warned! *Located in the heart of old Charlottetown.*

Rooms: 9: 4 kings, 4 queens and 1 double; all en suite, 3 with shower and separate jacuzzi, 3 bath/shower, 2 jacuzzi/shower and 1 with shower only.
Price: $135 – $295. No single rates.
Meals: Full breakfast included.
Directions: Take Highway 1a from Confederation Bridge into centre of Charlottetown. Turn right onto Fitzroy St, go 1.5 blocks. Shipwright Inn is on the right before Pownal St.

Map Number: 11

Woodlands Country Inn

Max Newby and Mary Cameron

RR 1, Cardigan C0A 1G0
Tel: 902-583-2275; toll-free 1-800-380-1562
Email: woodlands@pei.sympatico.ca Web: www.peisland.com/woodlands

Woodlands' reputation precedes it on two counts: Max's table-tennis skills and their maple syrup. I have to admit I was more interested in the latter, but if you reckon yourself a dab hand at table-tennis you should note that beating the host earns a free night. Built by local bigwig John Goff in 1841 and once an estate of 1000 acres, this sylvan oasis still sits among some of the old-world trees imported by Goff in the 1840s. It may have lost a few of its acres, but Woodlands still retains the grandeur of an old estate, although when Mary bought it in 1976 it had been empty for ten years and was a looted wreck. The house is full of *real* antiques. The English oak court-cupboard outside my room was 400 years old and my four-poster wouldn't have looked out of place in a medieval castle. This is the sort of house where you feel you really could discover Narnia through a forgotten wardrobe. Woodlands is a beautiful, tranquil place and a stroll down to the millstream through the woods is a must, as is a tour of the sugar shack. In bad weather Max's incredible record and video collection, plus their 2000-book library, should keep you entertained. A single night here just isn't long enough. *Beaches, golf, tennis and riding all within 10 minutes.*

Rooms: 3: 1 queen, 2 with both double and single; share 2 bathrooms (1 bath, 1 shower).
Price: $75 – $90 single or double occupancy. $15 for extra person. $225 for whole house. Seventh night is free.
Meals: Full breakfast included.
Directions: Follow Rte 311 from Cardigan, and Woodlands is on the right, 9 km after Cardigan's bridge. They're the first house after the Woodville Mills sign.
Closed: November to May.

Nova Scotia

The Lighthouse on Cape D'Or

Darcy Snell and Jenna Boon

PO Box 122, Advocate Harbour B0M 1A0
Tel: 902-670-0534
Email: capedor@hotmail.com Web: www.capedor.ca

After bumping further and further down a perilous dirt track in pounding rain and a particularly glutinous fog, it was with some elation that I spied the Lighthouse emerging through the gloom. I know how those stricken sailors must have felt. Yet such is the appeal of this maritime outpost that on this inclement Monday evening a gaggle of happy diners had made the journey. Once you've experienced it you'll understand why. Darcy was so wooed by the magic of the place that he pestered the local government for eight years before he got the lease. He'd neither stayed in a B&B nor cooked before, but he knew this tea-house could be transformed into something exceptional. Three years on and he's already had the *San Francisco Chronicle* billing it the 'best place to stay in Novia Scotia'. Not bad for a beginner, and I can see their point. Supper was a banquet of local offerings; memories of my unsavoury journey receding rapidly as I dined on scallops and wild blueberries. A short stumble away is the guesthouse, simple, stylish and with views to die for. The location is truly spectacular. Sitting up in bed it's as if you are suspended over the ocean, the waves crashing onto the rocks far below. Wild, remote, beautiful and casual, this is somewhere I'd like to spend much more time.

Rooms: 4: 1 queen, sitting area, en-suite shower; 1 double, private shower across hall; 2 doubles sharing bath and shower; 3 with ocean view, 1 cliffside view.
Price: $70 – $100 double occupancy. $65 – $80 single occ.
Meals: Full restaurant. All meals extra. Breakfast ranges from $4 to $8.
Directions: 6 km from the village of Advocate Harbour. Follow the blue signs – if you get lost, ask a local. 3 hours from Halifax and 2 hours from Amherst.
Closed: November 15th - May 1st.

Pelham House

Michael Boulter and Fay Paul

224 Pelham Street, PO Box 358, Lunenburg B0J 2C0
Tel: 902-634-7113; toll-free 1-800-508-0446 Fax: 902-634-7114
Email: pelham@ns.sympatico.ca Web: www.pelhamhouse.ca

A colourful abode in a quiet part of Lunenburg, Pelham House is a cheery, down-to-earth place that sets you up perfectly for the strains of a hard day's sightseeing. Two beautiful golden retrievers live here, as do Michael and Fay, but only the latter are allowed into guest areas. (Which is good news for you, by the way, because they are a lovely, chatty couple with a romantic history to make you smile.) The house is a bit different: wooden floors in various colours, vibrant rugs, lots of reds in the rooms downstairs. It's full of 'bits and bobs', as my notes so poetically describe the varied collections of objects that adorn the walls and shelves. There are display cabinets in the sitting room, collections of teapots in the dining room and toasters in the kitchen. And upstairs the corridor is festooned with platform signs from English railway stations and there's a saddle and two enormous, wooden toy cars.... Bedrooms boast eclectic mixtures of furniture and materials, and more of the painted wooden floors. This has been a B&B for ten years now, although only under the ministrations of Michael and Fay since late 1999. They visited Lunenburg the year before and were smitten. They say it has something to do with its similarity to a Scottish fishing village. I say it has something to do with Pelham House itself.

Rooms: 4: 1 king (converts to twins), 2 queens, 1 queen and twin; all en-suite bathrooms, 1 with whirlpool/shower, 2 with bath/sh, 1 with bath and sh.
Price: $85 – $125 single or double occupancy. $20 for extra person.
Meals: Full breakfast included.
Directions: From Hwy 103 take exit 10 (Mahone Bay) or 11 (Lunenburg) and follow signs to Lunenburg. At 3-way intersection in town go up hill on Lincoln St. Continue until Stop sign at Kempt. Turn right, then turn left at T-junction onto Pelham. House up on right.

Map Number: 11

Edgewater

Susan and Paul Seltzer

44 Mader's Cove Rd, RR 1, Mahone Bay B0J 2E0
Tel: 902-624-9382; toll-free 1-866-816-8688 Fax: 902-624-8733
Email: edgewater@bwr.eastlink.ca Web: www.bbcanada.com/116.html

It was when Paul wandered out onto the deck overlooking the small harbour and serenaded the twilight with his trombone that I surrendered completely to Edgewater's charms. The setting, the weather, the house at my back.... The (distant) neighbours finish gardening when they hear Paul play and guests consider where to eat. Mahone Bay is one of the prettiest towns in Canada, and three years ago the Seltzers were just another couple passing through. But you know how it is: you extend your holiday, you buy a B&B, you turn it into the best place around. They chose a spot outside town overlooking the water: in five minutes you can be at a restaurant, yet you return to serenity. They've got everything right inside as well. The removal of walls means that the dining area drifts into the sitting room and the music room. Upstairs, the three sizeable bedrooms are all stunners. (Other guests had already selected the loft suite ahead of these, so I can only guess at the delights there!) Downstairs, you'll notice the ingenious fireplace-cum-waterfall, before the simple colours, wooden floors, antiques and rugs confirm the wisdom of your choice. Come breakfast, you'll be feeling smugger still as Susan's creations work their indisputable magic; like me, you'll probably just sit and wonder at how very, very pleasant the whole experience is.

Rooms: 4: 1 king, 2 queens (1 in separate loft),
1 queen and twin; all have en-suite showers.
Price: $100 – $140 single or double occupancy.
$25 for extra person.
Meals: Full breakfast included.
Directions: Take exit 10 off Hwy 103 and go into
Mahone Bay, passing three churches on your right.
Turn left at the intersection in town and it's 2 miles
(just over 3 km) to the next left turn (Mader's Cove
Rd). The house is down here on the right.

Map Number: 11

Chimney Corner

Jan and Bob Wheeler

2581 Shore Road, Margaree Harbour B0E 2B0
Tel: 902-235-2104; toll-free 1-888-211-9061 Fax: 902-235-2104
Email: chimney.corner@ns.sympatico.ca
Web: www3.ns.sympatico.ca/chimney.corner

Jan and Bob spent months searching for this spot and 38 years after finding it, they're still tickled pink. They wanted somewhere secluded, with no road separating the property from the sea. Bob saw the land at a time when he was meant to be property-hunting in New England, but his new wife took the change of plan in her stride and they were soon Nova Scotians. Much wood-clearing created the property they had been craving, and peerless views of the Gulf of St Lawrence, served up in the most peaceful of atmospheres, are the result. You turn off the coast road a few kilometres south of the Cabot Trail and pass through a small wood before spying the Wheelers' wooden house at the end of the clearing. You can enjoy excellent B&B and your hosts' wise company here or, alternatively, there are two self-contained cottages above the house. The Wheelers' pride is The Cliff, which has few walls, much light and all creature comforts. Bob, who can build just about anything, has created look-out balconies a few metres from the cottages where you can watch the sea crashing on the rocks below. And if the water tempts you, there's a private beach shared with just two other houses.

Rooms: 2 B&B rooms: both queens; 1 private bath and shower, 1 en-suite bath/sh.
2 self-catering cottages: 1 double and 1 queen, with bath and shower.
Price: $100 for double occupancy B&B. $125 – $150 for the cottages. Singles less $10.
Meals: Full breakfast included for B&B rooms only.
Directions: From Cabot Trail, turn onto Route 219 at Margaree Harbour intersection and proceed along Shore Road for 7 km. From Inverness, turn off Route 19 to Route 219 at Dunvegan and continue north along Shore Road for 12 km.
Closed: November to May.

Map Number: 11

Louisbourg Harbour Inn

Parker and Suzanne Bagnell

9 Lower Warren St, Louisbourg B1C 1G6
Tel: 902-733-3222; toll-free 1-888-8888-466
Email: louisbourg@sprint.ca
Web: www.louisbourg.com/louisbourgharbourinn

This is the proverbial old sea captain's house, built 100 years ago by one Thomas Townsend. With delightful, salty views of Louisbourg Harbour, the islands and the fortress on the other side of the bay, you'll be congratulating Capt Townsend and reaching for the binoculars before you've unpacked your toothbrush. Parker's family have been in the area for years and he was raised in the house itself; nobody is more local. He took the building over from his parents, and a sympathetic extension helped create the sea-front inn that he and Suzanne wanted. From the pale yellow clapboard exterior to the hardwood floors and tranquil atmosphere, all is as it should be. A large first-floor ('second-floor' for you Canadians) balcony looks out over the wharves and you can watch crab and lobster fishermen unload their catch. Six of the rooms have harbour views. I rather liked Room 1, which has spruce floors, ivory walls, harbour view, side-balcony and bird-song, while Room 7, with windows on all sides and a two-person jacuzzi, is "great in a storm," says Parker. The inn was repeatedly recommended as I travelled around Nova Scotia and it's a pleasure to add my voice to the throng. *Louisbourg is a delightful old town and its fortress is a National Historic Site.*

Rooms: 8: all queens and all en suite. 5 have jacuzzi/shower; 1 has shower and 2 bath/shower.
Price: $105 – $180 double occupancy.
Meals: Full breakfast included.
Directions: Route 22 from Sydney becomes Louisbourg's main street. Turn left at the post office onto Lower Warren St and the inn is down on the left.
Closed: Mid-Oct - end May

Newfoundland

Quirpon Lighthouse Inn

Ed English
Quirpon Island A2H 6G1
Tel: toll-free 1-877-2546586 (1-877-2LINKUM) Fax: 709-639-1592
Email: quirpon@linkumtours.com
Web: www.linkumtours.com/f_inn.htm

This is the Real McCoy… a truly special, tell-the-grandchildren, buy-the film-rights kind of place providing the only inhabitation on Quirpon Island. The island juts out into the Atlantic off the northernmost tip of Newfoundland and has the longest iceberg-viewing season in the province. Time passes rapidly as you watch bergs and whales and enjoy the walks, views and splendid isolation. I actually saw very little the first day because of a real autumnal 'pea-souper', so waking up to the sun and the sea the next morning was all the more thrilling. You stay in one of two cottages, with the lighthouse (now functioning automatically) nearby. Inside, all is homely and warm; there is little luxury, but that's not why you're here. Your needs are met by a cheery local couple, Doris and Hubert Roberts. Doris cooks hearty meals to fuel your wanderings; Hubert is in charge of getting you to the island. They meet you at the dock in the tiny mainland village of Quirpon, and take you in a small fishing boat to the island's landing bay, from where there's a short moorland walk to the lighthouse. If the sea is rougher, you'll go to another bay and walk further (about one and a half hours). That's what happened to me, and yes, that's enormous fun too. Magical in every way. *Minimum two nights stay recommended.*

Rooms: 6 in main cottage: 4 queens, 2 singles; share 2 bath/shower. 4 in second cottage: 2 queens, 2 with 2 doubles; share 2 bath/shower.
Price: $250 – $350 double occupancy. $150 – $250 for singles. $50 for a child in a room. Price per day includes accomm, all meals and travel to and from island.
Meals: All meals included.
Directions: Travel north up Route 430. 10km before St Anthony turn L onto Route 436 (to L'Anse aux Meadows). After 20km turn R to Quirpon. Dock is 3km down here in the village – follow the signs.
Postal Address: PO Box 652, Corner Brook, NF, A2N 6G1.
Closed: November to April (open by very special arrangement).

Tuckamore

Barb Genge

PO Box 100, Main Brook A0K 3N0
Tel: 709-865-6361; toll-free 1-888-865-6361 Fax: 709-865-2112
Email: tuckamore.lodge@nf.sympatico.ca
Web: www.tuckamore-lodge.nf.net

This is another wonderful place to come and enjoy the majesty of the Canadian outdoors. Situated towards the tip of Newfoundland's Northern Peninsula, Tuckamore Lodge serves up wilderness, nature and rugged adventure on the friendliest of plates. Barb is the delightful soul of Tuckamore, which she has been running for 17 years, and the welcome is genuine. This is what Newfoundland is all about. If you're not "m' dear" within a day of arriving, you should probably check your breath. Time here can be spent in a hundred different ways. Hiking, fishing, kayaking, whale-, iceberg-, moose- and bird-watching, boat tours and Viking-related excursions are available in the summer, while all manner of snow-related activities fill up the winter. September and October are the main hunting months. Accommodation is provided in one of two buildings: the older, A-frame, pine lodge has four guest rooms, and the new cedar lodge with its lofty ceiling has eight more (try to get a room upstairs here). Meals are served at big communal tables in both the lodges – prepare your stories – while bedrooms are mostly wood-walled, chalet-style affairs with pine-log beds and colourful duvets; fine places to collapse after the rigours of a day of heady Newfie air.

Rooms: 12: 4 in main building: all with en/s showers, 3 with 2 double beds and 1 with queen. 8 in other lodge: mix of queens and doubles, all en/s bath or shower.

Price: $110 – $170 double occ. Singles $100 – $120.

Meals: Full breakfast included. Lunch at $12 – $15 and dinner at $30 from set menu. Beer and wine extra.

Directions: North on Route 430, turn right onto 432 towards Main Brook. Left after 53 km. Go another 33 km and when you see water on your right look left for the driveway.

Map Number: 12

BlueWater Lodge and Retreat

Gary and Winifred Sargent
PO Box 1449, Lewisporte A0G 3A0
Tel: 709-424-4600 Fax: 709-424-4600
Email: bluewater@nf.sympatico.ca Web: www.relax-at-bluewater.ca

A genuine wilderness retreat, BlueWater is somewhere to turn off the cell phone, loosen the collar and get out the nature guide. The imposing, white-cedar lodge rises up from the trees at the eastern extreme of Newfoundland's boreal forests and is surrounded by spruce, fir, cherry, maple, aspen and birch. You'll be identifying them all by the time you leave. The large deck looks out towards Indian Arm Pond (although if that's a pond, then I'm a midget) and there is no other property for miles. This is not a place for agoraphobes! The Sargents designed the building and laid the gravel road without ever compromising the natural splendour. Winifred is the interior force, designing rooms and creating meals, while Gary, who worked for Parks Canada in Alberta, builds, grows and generally asserts order in nature's midst. He's one of those vastly knowledgeable, easy-going guys who will have you hooked on the wild before you realise it. Soaring wood ceilings and massive log walls – no need for further insulation – characterise the main room, while the chalet-style bedrooms have home-made beds, wooden floors and panelling in many different types of wood. This is a new operation and the Sargents' enthusiasm is contagious. You have been warned! *Activities include hiking, canoeing, cross-country skiing and extreme relaxing.*

Rooms: 10: 5 doubles, 5 twins; all have en-suite showers.
Price: $115 – $125 double occupancy. Singles $105 – $115.
Meals: Full breakfast included. Dinner (set menu) by prior arrangement. 3 courses from $29 per person, but cheaper if booked with accommodation.
Directions: Situated just off the Trans-Canada Highway, the driveway to BlueWater is 3 km east of the Route 340 intersection (which heads to Lewisporte).

Map Number: 12

Fishers' Loft Inn

John and Peggy Fisher
PO Box 36, Port Rexton A0C 2H0
Tel: 709-464-3240; toll-free 1-877-464-3240 Fax: 709-464-3240
Email: enquiries@fishersloft.com Web: www.fishersloft.com

This beautiful inn sits on a coastal hillside overlooking Trinity Bay and the inlets and saltbox houses spread out below. In the middle of summer, you can watch icebergs and whales bobbing past; in September, when I was there, you'll probably have to content yourself (it's pretty easy) with admiring the play of sea, mist, sun and rock. It really is spectacular. John and Peggy had a summer home here for many years before moving permanently in 1990, and after a glorious night and still more glorious morn, I was tempted to follow suit. The main buildings are new, but the style is old Newfoundland. Pale bedrooms have large windows and painted wooden floors, and all feels authentic. Downstairs, windows surround the dining room, eliciting a chorus of happy sighs from those admiring the breakfast-time view. Only food of the highest order could compete and the inn responds to the challenge, as local staff produce wonderful dishes, many cooked with exotic twists. At supper, I had salmon nori (a Japanese style) and smacked my lips for weeks after. The Fishers are a delightful couple with the right ideas about how to treat their guests – they would never force you into any contrived gaiety for example. Fiercely proud of Newfoundland, they love to show off its diversity to visitors (including Judi Dench and Kevin Spacey who stayed here during the filming of *The Shipping News*). *In the area: theatre festival, movie set, coastal hikes, kayaking.*

Rooms: 12: 10 queens and 2 twins; 4 have sitting room as well; all have en-suite bath/shower.
Price: $110 – $220 for single or double occupancy.
Meals: Full breakfast available but not included. Dinner by reservation in the restaurant ($39 – $45 per person). Dining/accommodation packages available.
Directions: Leave the Trans-Canada Highway at Clarenville and take Route 230 to Port Rexton. Once in the village, follow the signs to Fishers' Loft.
Closed: November 1st to May 1st.

Map Number: 12

NaGeira House Bed & Breakfast Inn

Diana and Marvin Dove

7 Musgrave St, Carbonear A1Y 1B4
Tel: 709-596-1888; toll-free 1-800-600-7757 Fax: 709-596-4622
Email: nageirahouse@nf.aibn.com Web: www.nageirahouse.com

Sheila NaGeira, a 17th-century Irish princess, would be delighted to know that she'd given a name to this splendid B&B. She was kidnapped by pirates and taken to Carbonear, but the area has plenty of attractions to reward a voluntary visit. Foremost among these is NaGeira itself, with its panelled interiors, comfy sofas and large, simply-coloured bedrooms. Wood abounds, be it the Canadian maple in the hallway and dining room, oak and mahogany panelling elsewhere, the recently restored staircase, or outside in the form of the towering chestnuts and birches beside the house. There is nothing heavy about the look though: lots of light and clever use of pale paint tones prevent that. Upstairs, the four bedrooms lead off the corners of the landing, and all have down-filled duvets, earth-tone walls and dark wood doors. The large Room 1, with its spectacular mustard bedspread, textured walls and jacuzzi, is the most popular, while the less ebullient colours and four-poster in Room 3 will be more to some tastes. Diana and Marvin grew up in Newfoundland, but left the island years ago. They were running a sheep farm in Ontario when the siren call of their homeland grew too strong and in 2002 they bought NaGeira (already a successful B&B) and set about adding another strand to the island's tradition of hospitality.

Rooms: 4: 1 king, 2 queens, 1 double with single; all en-suite bathrooms, 1 with jacuzzi and shower, 2 with bath/shower, 1 with shower.
Price: $70 – $159 double occupancy. Singles less $10.
Meals: Full breakfast included. Dinner by reservation, 4 people minimum. $32 per person for 3 courses.
Directions: Entering Carbonear from the south on Route 70, turn right at the lights and follow the road around the bay. Continue past Ultramar gas station and turn left up Musgrave St. House is on the left.

Indexes

Index by town name

Index by house name

THE GREENWOOD GUIDE TO
AUSTRALIA & NEW ZEALAND

special hand-picked accommodation

The second title in the Greenwood Guides series offers you the chance to follow our many footsteps across both these countries.

We have chosen 192 of the friendliest B&Bs, farms, lodges, wilderness camps and small hotels covering the whole of Australia and New Zealand.

We are dividing the two countries into two books for the second edition, both due for publication in October 2003. For information or to order any of our books see our website at www.greenwoodguides.com, or email us at editor@greenwoodguides.com.